When I read *A Grand Way to Live*, I was struck by how every one of the ninety devotions feeds my deepest desire: to impact my grandchildren so they and their descendants will be in heaven with me! This book provided me with direction—both from Scripture and from a practical perspective—to be intentional about passing my faith along. Grandparent, if your desire is the same, you'll find inspiration and guidance in each devotion! My wife and I will read through them together. Why don't you join us?

—*Larry Fowler*
Founder, Legacy Coalition

Grandparents: you have a valuable opportunity in front of you as you begin this devotional book by Jay Payleitner. You'll find eye-opening insights and practical tips on every page. Even at "grandparent age," there's still a lot you must learn, and that will happen as you read. You'll also smile a lot. You'll be encouraged and challenged in two of the most important aspects of your life: being an engaged and engaging grandparent, and being called to deeper fellowship with God. You can also use this book as an opportunity to gather with other grandparents, support one another, and pray for each other as you make vital contributions to the next generation.

—*Dr. Ken Canfield*
Founder, National Association for Grandparenting
Host, *Grandkids Matter Radio*
Author, *7 Secrets of Effective Fathers* and *The Heart of Grandparenting*

Jay Payleitner has taken a "plateful of spaghetti"—i.e., grandparenting wisdom—and laid it out one strand at a time in a ninety-day digestible and compelling devotional. Read it and you'll be inspired to become the best possible grandparenting version of yourself...and more! You'll also develop a heart overflowing with gratefulness that, all along, God created you to be Gramps, Chief, Mimi, Gammy...or whatever special name your grandchildren have chosen to call you.

—*Valerie Bell*
CEO Emerita, Awana Clubs International
Founding board member, Legacy Coalition

Jay provides practical and, most importantly, actionable advice for grandparents. Drawing on his life experiences and his role as the creative strategist for Christian Grandparenting New York, he shares valuable wisdom on how grandparents can be a loving and guiding influence in their grandchildren's lives. Each devotion offers an opportunity to nurture a child's faith in Christ and create joyful, lasting memories that strengthen the bond between grandparent and grandchild. Isn't that what every grandparent hopes for? I highly recommend this wonderful devotional!

—*Lee Ann Mancini*
Founder, Raising Christian Kids, Inc.
Award-winning author, *Raising Kids to Follow Christ*

A Grand Way to Live equips you for what may be your most important role and your highest calling in life—being a grandparent. Jay Payleitner brings a wealth of experience and insight, delivered in readable—sometimes entertaining, sometimes poignant—doses. Expect to walk away from each day's reading with a right-now idea that will help you bring eternal good into precious young lives.

—*Dwight Clough*
Author, *How to Fix Everything*
Founder, EmpowerGood.com community

Jay Payleitner's writing is practical, playful, and profoundly grounded in biblical truth. *A Grand Way to Live* isn't just a devotional for grandparents. It's a blueprint for legacy, a call to faithfulness, and a joyful reminder that it's never too late to live on mission. I know a life-giving book when I see it. This is one.

—*Ken Gonyer*
Former CEO, Choice Books

As a new grandparent myself, I know Jay's book will be a valuable resource! It is more than a devotional. Yes, it is packed with applicable Scripture, but the book is also full of stories with practical applications and valuable tips, including some indispensable warnings. *A Grand Way to Live* is a must-have for any grandparent!

—*Scott Haima*
Executive Director, National Coalition of Ministries to Men

Jay Payleitner understands what it means to be what we call a "great" grandparent—one who is called and equipped to love, pray, serve, coach, and model God's grace to their grandchildren. By doing those things, we also become "grand-partners" with their parents—our adult children—and with their spouses, assisting them in many different ways. Although that list of duties may make grandparenting seem difficult, even impossible, *"with God all things are possible"* (Matthew 19:26). We believe Jay's devotions will be great resources for recharging your grandparenting batteries and helping you rely on God for wisdom and empowerment each and every day!

—*Paul and Diana Miller*
Authors, *A Guide to Great Grandparenting* and *A Parents' Guide to Great Grand-Partnering*
GrandCamp Coordinators and board members, Christian Grandparenting Network

The world desires to keep you at the status quo. Wonderfully, these thought-provoking devotions from my friend Jay Payleitner will challenge you to be a better person and more effective grandparent, while directing all the glory to our Lord and Savior, Jesus! *A Grand Way to Live* certainly lives up to its title.

—*Darren Bailey*
Republican nominee for governor of Illinois, 2022
Author, *Rooted for a Reason*
Third-generation farmer and grandfather of thirteen

Jay Payleitner delivers again! Our nine grandkids call us Papa and Granny. What an incredible privilege and responsibility it is to speak into their lives! I am continually motivated to be the kind of Papa that my grandpa Tiede was to me and my dad was to our four kids! I am always looking for help! Jay Payleitner comes to the rescue with *A Grand Way to Live*—ninety devotions filled with Scripture and great ideas for things you and I can do with our grandkids. But Jay does not just share ideas—in every chapter, he asks a very powerful question: "What about you?" Jay doesn't want you to just read his book and say, "Nice ideas!"—Jay wants you and me to actually act on those ideas! Your grandkids will love it! One day, they will be telling their grandkids about the times they had with you!

—*Bob Tiede*
US Leadership Development Team, Cru
Blogger, LeadingWithQuestions.com

Two years ago, Janna and I became grandparents, and now we have three beautiful granddaughters with the expectation that this number will grow in the years ahead. It has been said, "Grandkids are your reward for not killing your own," and is this statement prophetic. Jay's book *A Grand Way to Live* offers practical insights on how to become better at grandparenting than we were at parenting.

In essence, we get a do-over opportunity to invest in our children's children. What a joy and a blessing it is to be actively involved in the lives of our grandchildren.

—*Rod Handley*
Author and speaker
Founder and president, Character That Counts

It is not often that I find the kind of practical, creative devotional materials that Jay Payleitner has provided in this collection for grandparents. Jay understands that the heart of the messenger is just as important as the message. That's why these devotions not only focus on how to have conversations and engaging moments that matter with your grandchildren (and children) but also challenge you to cultivate a heart after God so that another generation can actually smell the aroma of Christ in you. Practical, creative, real, convicting...these devotions combine all these elements for maximum generation-to-generation impact.

—Cavin T. Harper
Founder, Christian Grandparenting Network
Founder and executive director, ElderQuest Ministries
Author and international speaker

A
GRAND
WAY
TO LIVE

A 90-Day Devotional

A GRAND WAY TO LIVE

Faith, Wisdom, and Joy for Every Grandparent

JAY PAYLEITNER

WHITAKER HOUSE

A GRAND WAY TO LIVE
Faith, Wisdom, and Joy for Every Grandparent (A 90-Day Devotional)

jaypayleitner.com

ISBN: 979-8-88769-393-4
eBook ISBN: 979-8-88769-394-1
Printed in the United States of America
© 2025 by Jay Payleitner

Whitaker House
1030 Hunt Valley Circle
New Kensington, PA 15068
www.whitakerhouse.com

Library of Congress Control Number: 2025904200

1 2 3 4 5 6 7 8 9 10 11 Ⱳ 32 31 30 29 28 27 26 25

CONTENTS

FOREWORD

Our eleven grandchildren call my wife, Dottie, "Grammy" or "G," and I love every moment of watching her in that role. Being a grandmother isn't just something she does—it's who she is. The moment those kids tumble out of the car or burst through our front door, calling her name, Dottie lights up. With effortless warmth, she greets them with hugs, kisses, and boundless love. It's a beautiful thing to witness.

As "Papa," I'm right there beside her, yet I'm still in awe. While Dottie loves without hesitation or limits, I find myself analyzing and thinking about God's design for grandparents and how it differs from being a parent. I believe both roles hold tremendous value when we humbly open our hearts to God's compassion and grace. Luke 1:50 assures us, *"His mercy extends to those who fear him, from generation to generation."*

I think back to the six-point checklist for parents I developed years ago: Affirmation. Acceptance. Appreciation. Availability. Affection. Accountability. For grandparents, all those boxes still need to be checked, but the application is different. Sometimes, we step in to fill the gaps; other times, we simply reinforce what parents have already begun.

In most families, time with grandkids is limited, and it's the parents who are the main source of discipline and setting expectations. On the other hand, when we are with our grandchildren, we likely have fewer distractions, allowing us to be fully present so that we may nurture deep connections. That makes grandparents an exceptional source of availability, appreciation, and affection.

For example, imagine your four-year-old granddaughter proudly presents you with a bouquet of dandelions. You would take the time to gush over that gift and express your gratitude with physical hugs and words of love, and maybe even find a vase for those cheerful little weeds! A busy parent might be less enthusiastic.

Whether it comes to them naturally or not, grandparents need to be intentional about building relationships with their grandkids. In your quest to foster trust and connection, that "Six A" checklist may come in handy. Every grandchild needs to know that "Grandma and Grandpa really love me!"

When your grandchildren's hearts are full, the natural flow of life will present many opportunities for you to turn the conversation toward God's love and purpose for their young lives. With that foundation, you become a trusted resource for honest and heartfelt answers—which means that, from the toddler years through adulthood, they will feel comfortable coming to you with spiritual questions. And that's a good thing! Especially if you are ready and grounded in God's truth yourself.

That's why a book like this is so important. Walking through these devotions—on your own, with your grandparenting partner, or alongside like-minded seniors—will equip you for those meaningful (and sometimes challenging) conversations with those young ones you love so much. As a bonus, these short, thought-provoking chapters might just give a gentle nudge to your own spiritual growth.

—Josh D. McDowell
International speaker, apologist, and author, and Papa

INTRODUCTION

Let your light shine before others, that they may see your good deeds and glorify your Father in heaven.
—Matthew 5:16

Rita and I have eight grandchildren who call us "Grama" and "Chief." One of our grandchildren bounding through our front door, calling out one of those names, is the greatest sound in the world. I hope you regularly have that kind of experience.

Those eight young lives have reminded me that I need to be a servant leader to my family. Above all, that means honoring, elevating, and reflecting the love of God, especially to those grandkids.

If it were a gargantuan task, I'd still steadfastly shoulder that responsibility. But you know what? That goal is not as difficult as you may think.

Grandma and Grandpa, just follow your instincts. Let the Holy Spirit lead. You've been prepping for this role your entire life. Every lesson you've learned, every peak and valley you've experienced, and all the love you've felt have prepared you for the wonderment, chaos, and adventure of grandparenting.

You're ready.

Just to remind you, reflecting God's love to your grandchildren begins with being in their lives and modeling Christ in you. (See Galatians 2:20.) Only then can you speak into their lives with humble words of gratitude and grace.

Let's all agree that being pious and preachy or constantly sermonizing is ultimately ineffective (or even counterproductive). Still, your grandkids should know that your faith is important to you. They need to know you read your Bible, go to church, and have a circle of Christian friends who invest in your life on a regular basis.

They need to see you shining the light of Christ into this dark world by loving God, your neighbor, and yourself. Harvesting the fruit of the Spirit as you convey love, joy, peace, patience, kindness, goodness, faithfulness, gentleness, and self-control. (See Galatians 5:22–23.) And, yes, welcoming every member of your family into your home and authentically enjoying your interactions.

These ninety devotions will help with all of that. You'll also find practical strategies for catching fireflies, building elephants, sprinkling stardust, honoring creation, defying cultural expectations, uncovering your grandchildren's talents, being a blessing to your kids, and even making the most of holidays.

Keep reading—maybe with a book club or group of friends—and you can also look forward to lessons in how to be less grumpy, when to zip your lip, and why you need to ask permission before giving advice. I've included other surprises too.

Presenting *A Grand Way to Live: Faith, Wisdom, and Joy for Every Grandparent.*

All from a biblical perspective.

All to build a legacy of faith so that, one day, you will be there to welcome your grandchildren into heaven.

Won't that be great?

DAY 1
LET US BE TREES

So then, just as you received Christ Jesus as Lord,
continue to live your lives in him, rooted and built up in him,
strengthened in the faith as you were taught,
and overflowing with thankfulness.
—Colossians 2:6–7

Are you rooted, built up, and strengthened in Him? That's the season we're in.

We were once seedlings like our grandchildren, easily trampled. Soon enough, we grew into mere saplings with shallow roots and paper-thin bark.

Now, as mature trees, we drink deeply from nearby streams, anchored by strong roots, producing fruit in abundance. Our craggy bark is impenetrable to the storms of life. Our arching branches provide home and sustenance. Our leaves turn gold, then crimson, and fall to earth, enriching and nurturing generations of healthy growth.

As grandparents, our primary responsibility is to stand tall as trustworthy symbols of strength, protection, and provision. Pointing skyward to the Creator.

What's more, we have become humbly aware that the cycle of life will one day call us back to the soil, confident that our legacy fosters new life, new growth, and new fruit.

You may recognize this imagery from the first three verses of the book of Psalms:

Blessed is the one who does not walk in step with the wicked or stand in the way that sinners take or sit in the company of mockers, but whose delight is in the law of the Lord, and who meditates on his law day and night. That person is like a tree planted by streams of water, which yields its fruit in season and whose leaf does not wither—whatever they do prospers.

(Psalm 1:1–3)

If that metaphor seems a bit too poetic for your taste, no worries. However, you must admit that you love the idea that *"whatever [you] do prospers."*

To prosper, you need a plan that includes "not walking with the wicked" and "delighting in the law of the Lord."

When it comes to your grandchildren, the plan to prosper requires you to be present in ways that delight and invite. With your adult children, it means getting on the same page and strengthening your relationship.

Finally, essential to your plan is resting in the secure knowledge that God will one day say, *"Well done, my good and faithful servant"* (Matthew 25:21 NLT).

All that is to say: may your roots run deep and your harvest be plentiful.

WHAT ABOUT YOU?

Maybe you don't immediately see yourself as a tree. But God's Word employs all kinds of metaphors for believers. You've read passages and heard sermons that call us to be salt and light, living stones, molded clay, branches of the vine, living temples, persevering athletes, and sheep. (See Matthew 5:13–14; 1 Peter 2:5; Isaiah 64:8; John 15:5; 1 Corinthians 6:19, 9:24–25; and Psalm 23.)

By the way, your grandchildren are also called to be all these things. Bookmark this page so you'll know where to begin your Bible study and prayer for them. And with them!

DANDELIONS, CATERPILLARS, AND PINECONES

Jesus said, "Let the little children come to me,
and do not hinder them,
for the kingdom of God belongs to such as these."
—Matthew 19:14

When's the last time you made an exciting discovery? Well, your grandkids are learning something wondrous and new every day. A child's natural curiosity will continue for years until someone or something compels them to stop. Sometimes busy parents can inadvertently become that killjoy. They just don't have time to answer all the silly, repetitive, and fantastical questions their little ones ask. Before long, those questions stop. Tragically, so might the curiosity behind them.

It's a real loss. Parents of preschoolers don't realize that, years from now, they would absolutely cherish the opportunity to answer questions from that same child as a young adult.

All this is one more reason grandparents exist!

We know how important it is to *"let the little children come"* (Matthew 19:14) with their discoveries and questions. When they bring us a dandelion, caterpillar, or pinecone, we don't dismiss their gift .

When they ask about rainbows, clouds, or constellations, grandparents are more likely to seize the moment, engaging in an eye-opening dialogue that points to the Creator of the universe. With a bit of forethought, you can have God's Word ready to paint the picture of His creation and glory.

The heavens declare the glory of God; the skies proclaim the work of his hands.   (Psalm 19:1)

Whenever I bring clouds over the earth and the rainbow appears in the clouds, I will remember my covenant between me and you and all living creatures of every kind.

(Genesis 9:14–15)

Let the heavens rejoice, let the earth be glad; let the sea resound, and all that is in it. Let the fields be jubilant, and everything in them; let all the trees of the forest sing for joy.

(Psalm 96:11–12)

Let's not blame Mom and Dad if they don't yet appreciate the wonder of children making discoveries and asking questions. That's something we all had to learn. Also, don't beat up on yourself if you are just now realizing you didn't make enough time for your own children. That kind of guilt is a wasted emotion unless it motivates you to seek out time with your grandchildren—in nature, away from screens, one-on-one when possible.

Applaud the inquisitive nature of future generations. Never dismiss their curiosity. Join in their discoveries. If you let it happen, your grandchildren may see the world—and you—in a brand-new way. Through their eyes, you just might also make some new discoveries about the glory of creation.

WHAT ABOUT YOU?

Grandparents can be the ones who rescue a child's imagination from being stifled or discouraged. When they bring you a dandelion, caterpillar, or pinecone, don't just thank them. Marvel at the gift. Ask questions. Stop and think about puffballs, butterflies, and pine trees, and you'll realize that all three represent God's promise for the future. That's a lesson only you have the time, patience, and awareness to share.

SEASONED SPEECH

*Remember not only to say the right thing in the right place, but
far more difficult still,
to leave unsaid the wrong thing at the tempting moment.*
—Benjamin Franklin[1]

As a grandparent, you've seen a lot. You've got a lifetime of experience, an opinion on just about everything, and you're almost always right. However, that doesn't mean you should proclaim yourself to be the expert on all that is good and true and tell everything you know to everyone you meet the instant you meet them. You may have already discovered that this kind of know-it-all attitude doesn't always sit well with the next generation. By the way, you're not infallible and have not personally cornered the market on truth.

Colossians 4:6 confirms that we should present our words—especially our testimony—thoughtfully and respectfully. Paul wrote, *"Let your conversation be always full of grace, seasoned with salt, so that you may know how to answer everyone."* Did you get that? The goal is for your words to be "tasty"—grace-filled and nicely seasoned. Plus, your words need to take into consideration that each person with whom you're talking is in a different place, with different temperaments, and facing different challenges. That kind of heart-to-heart understanding only happens after you have been holding your tongue, listening carefully, and investing enough time to craft a thoughtful response.

Of course, the blossoming generations need to hear your wisdom. The lessons you learned the hard way can help them avoid the mistakes you made. What a gift that can be! Indeed, that's one of the reasons your children and grandchildren need you in their lives. But your

---

1. "Benjamin Franklin Quotes," BrainyQuote, https://www.brainyquote.com/quotes/benjamin_franklin_121174.

worthwhile advice and wise counsel will never even be considered if the words are delivered with a pompous edge, a nasty bitterness, or, perhaps worse, a syrupy sweetness that causes any message of grace and truth to be hard to swallow.

Let's prioritize lightly seasoned speech.

WHAT ABOUT YOU?

Consider some of the most recent conversations you've had with your grandchildren. Did you listen before offering instruction? Did you bestow empathy before correcting or chastising? Actually, with your grandkids, it may be a little easier because they are so innocent and lovable. A bigger challenge might be to consider your most recent interactions with your adult children and their spouses. Did you listen to what they were really saying? Was your response well-seasoned, respectful, and spoken in love? Sometimes we forget that they are adults and the primary caretakers of our grandchildren and should be treated as such.

PRAY FOR THEM BY NAME

The one who enters by the gate is the shepherd of the sheep. The
gatekeeper opens the gate for him,
and the sheep listen to his voice.
He calls his own sheep by name and leads them out.
—John 10:2–3

In the parable of the Good Shepherd, the sheep know Jesus's voice. That's not surprising. What is surprising is that He calls them by name. Do sheep have names? Apparently so!

In any case, your grandchildren have names. Do you pray for them by name? Do you lift them up as individuals? Your intervention on their behalf is one way you can help them discover their unique gifts and talents. Picture each face. Imagine what they are doing this very minute. It doesn't matter whether they are down the street, across the country, on some mission field, or even playing video games in the basement of your own crowded house.

Every child you're thinking of right now faces critical turning points during every season of life. That's the nature of this fallen world. Babies and toddlers are learning about love, trust, and fear. Your school-age grandchildren are surrounded by conflicting values. Older grandchildren may feel pressure trying to fit in at the big state university or finding the time and energy to tuck their kids into bed.

Stop right now and pray that God will hold each of your precious grandchildren in the palm of His hand. It's worth remembering that He loves them even more than you do.

I'm convinced that visualizing each grandchild and praying in specifics helps you track how and when each prayer is answered, as well as helps you reflect on how you may be part of the answer to that prayer. Picturing each sweet, smirky, smudged, grimacing, or shining face as you pray will connect your heart to their heart and to the heart of Jesus.

This doesn't have to be some long, laborious burden. It's just an exercise in staying aware of what your grandchildren are going through and turning your heart and theirs to God. Maybe pray something like this:

Dear Lord, please help Zachary in his moral choices. Help Makayla discover her gifts. Help Peyton see You as the God of second chances. Help Wyatt feel Your unconditional love. Help Cooper come face-to-face with the sin in his life. Help young Claire meet You at an early age. Help Colton find some solid Christian friends at his new school. Help Brooke and her new boyfriend, Parker, to take it slow. Bless Lily and Mason's upcoming wedding and marriage. If Savannah is called to a life of singleness, help her and her parents know that can be a God-honoring choice. Amen.

WHAT ABOUT YOU?

Can you do this? Can you lift each grandchild up by name, picture each face, imagine where they are this very moment, and be part of the process that covers them with God's love? Those fifteen minutes—could be the most rewarding part of your day...and theirs.

THE NEEDLEPOINT METAPHOR

*"For my thoughts are not your thoughts, neither are your
ways my ways," declares the* Lord. *"As the heavens are higher
than the earth, so are my ways higher than your ways and my
thoughts than your thoughts."*
—Isaiah 55:8–9

If you happen to be a grandma (or grandpa) who does cross-stitch
or needlepoint, this may be the most valuable devotion in this entire
book. You'll be reminded of its deep truth whenever you pick up your
needle and thread. Even if you don't know your knit from your purl,
keep reading. The needlepoint metaphor is a lesson worth knowing
and passing on.

Imagine a young lad sitting at the foot of his grandmother's
rocking chair. The fireplace is crackling, and she's relaxing with some
embroidery after a long day. The boy looks up quizzically as his
grandma's hands move the needle in and through the delicate tapes-
try. What does he see? From below, her handiwork looks like a form-
less, purposeless, tangled zigzag of knots and loose threads. But when
the boy says, "Whatcha doin', Grammy?" she smiles and tilts the top
of the embroidery hoop toward the boy to reveal a charming garden
scene outlined by a few well-chosen words of wisdom.

The view from below is confusing; the view from above makes
perfect sense.

It is just like that when we compare our perspective with God's.
Many parts of our messy lives are filled with loose threads, zigzags,
and knots. There are times when we have lost our way, changed our
minds, and stopped in our tracks. But a heavenly perspective—one
we cannot possibly have yet—reveals perfect order.

At the end of our lives, we'll see how God's handiwork has come together in complete perfection. Until then, we'll have to trust the Creator to keep crafting the story of our lives. Occasionally, we'll get a glimpse of His entire plan, but only if we rest at His feet, lift our eyes with trust and expectation, and say, "Whatcha doin', Papa?"

It's a great word picture and a visual image you should definitely share with your grandchildren. But when? Consider being intentional about sharing that lesson the next time you see them, while it's fresh in your heart and mind. Maybe save that lesson for when they ask why bad things happen to good people. You'll probably remember it when you happen to pass a wall of framed cross-stitch, walking with your grandchild past the craft booths at the county fair. Certainly, you'll compellingly share this metaphor if and when they enter a room in which you're doing some needlepoint.

It's such a wonderful lesson that it might be a reason for any Grammy or Gramps to take up a new hobby!

WHAT ABOUT YOU?

First and foremost, take this lesson into your own heart. God knows what He's doing. He sees the big picture. You can trust Him.

Also, never forget that you have stored up dozens of great spiritual lessons. Your grandkids need to hear just about all of them. Those teachable moments come when you least expect them. Don't miss them. Take full advantage. That's another reason why you need to be intentional about just sharing life with your grandkids.

A MEDITATION ON GENERATIONS

Open my eyes that I may see wonderful things in your law.
—Psalm 119:18

The word "grandparent" shows up just once in the *New International Version* translation of the Bible. In 1 Timothy 5:4, Paul seems to be instructing younger generations to take care of Grandma after Grandpa dies. The verse reads, *"But if a widow has children or grandchildren, these should learn first of all to put their religion into practice by caring for their own family and so repaying their parents and grandparents, for this is pleasing to God."*

The term "children's children" shows up five times in the *New International Version*. That includes the hopeful psalm sung at Israelite marriages—*"May you live to see your children's children"* (Psalm 128:6)—and also the ominous vow to Israel when they had forsaken God and were worshipping idols: *"'Therefore I bring charges against you again,' declares the LORD. 'And I will bring charges against your children's children'"* (Jeremiah 2:9).

The pages in this devotional confirm that God cares greatly about you, your children, and your grandchildren. But also—as noted in Scripture—they show how God confirms both positive and negative generational impact.

Perhaps not surprisingly, according to my online concordance, the word "generation" or "generations" appears more than 230 times in my trusty NIV. If you're web savvy, you may want to do a passage search following this theme on BibleGateway.com. Once you start, you may never stop. Examples follow:

I will establish my covenant as an everlasting covenant between me and you and your descendants after you for the generations to come, to be your God and the God of your descendants after you. (Genesis 17:7)

Celebrate the Festival of Unleavened Bread, because it was on this very day that I brought your divisions out of Egypt. Celebrate this day as a lasting ordinance for the generations to come. (Exodus 12:17)

He remembers his covenant forever, the promise he made, for a thousand generations. (1 Chronicles 16:15)

Then we your people, the sheep of your pasture, will praise you forever; from generation to generation we will proclaim your praise. (Psalm 79:13)

And Mary said: "My soul glorifies the Lord and my spirit rejoices in God my Savior, for he has been mindful of the humble state of his servant. From now on all generations will call me blessed, for the Mighty One has done great things for me—holy is his name." (Luke 1:46–49)

Now to him who is able to do immeasurably more than all we ask or imagine, according to his power that is at work within us, to him be glory in the church and in Christ Jesus throughout all generations, for ever and ever! Amen. (Ephesians 3:20–21)

Later in these pages, you'll dig deeper into other biblical passages that reference the generational impact of grandparenting. I promise that you'll appreciate both the trustworthy consistency of Scripture and also how it never fails to provide surprising discoveries.

WHAT ABOUT YOU?

On this side of heaven, you will never know just how many members of future generations you've impacted through your love, faithfulness, and courageous intercession on behalf of your children and grandchildren.

MODELING IMPERFECTION

If we claim to be without sin, we deceive ourselves and the truth
is not in us. If we confess our sins,
he is faithful and just and will forgive us our sins and purify us
from all unrighteousness.
—1 John 1:8–9

As grandparents, we see ourselves as role models. In general, that's a good thing. As we share life lessons, the practice of demonstrating how to live is often much more effective than delivering an overbearing lecture. Grandparents should take every opportunity to model proper manners, good sportsmanship, how to roll out a pie crust, and how to pound a nail.

Nevertheless, sometimes our attempts to be a role model can backfire.

Ken Davis, a nationally known clean comedian, recalls how he would mistakenly create a "perception of perfection"[2] with his children and grandchildren. On a recent podcast interview with Legacy Coalition, Davis said, "I tried to make sure they saw me as someone who didn't do anything wrong. And I did not create grandchildren or children who didn't do anything wrong. I created children and grandchildren who hid the things they had done wrong from me."[3]

Realizing his mistake, Davis was motivated to acknowledge his own imperfections and began using words and phrases young people need to hear from grandparents:

2. Wayne Rice and John Coulombe, hosts, *Legacy Grandparenting*, season 2, episode 18, "Confessions of an Unintentional Grandparent featuring Ken Davis," Legacy Coalition, December 30, 2022, 29 min., 15 sec., https://legacycoalition. com/podcast.
3. Rice and Coulombe, "Unintentional Grandparent," at 29:18–37.

"I'm sorry."

"I was wrong."

"I want you to know, honey, I'm not perfect."

Soon, the humorist and grandfather saw firsthand how speaking words of confession can plant a seed in the heart of a grandchild. Before you know it, the young people in your life will discover that the empowering gift of forgiveness is readily available, from person to person and from a loving God.

Admitting our own brokenness to our kids and grandkids is not a sign of weakness. It's acknowledging that we're human—to be transparent and confess our need for a Savior. It's the first step of repentance and even key to battling the dangers of legalism. Children who understand they can never be perfect are free to live, love, learn, make mistakes, and not hide their sins. They realize they can go to their parents, grandparents, and God in humility and say, "I messed up. Help me do better."

That's a good reminder for Christians of all ages.

WHAT ABOUT YOU?

It's tempting, isn't it? Our life experience has given us skills and schemes that we might use to cover our tracks and hide our mistakes. But let's not go there. Our adult children can see right through us anyway, so let's not even try to present ourselves as faultless. When it comes to our grandchildren, we definitely want them to look up to us as role models. However, one of the best things we can demonstrate—even more important than baking and carpentry—is how to turn to God for forgiveness.

ASK THEM TO PRAY FOR YOU

For where two or three gather in my name,
there am I with them.
—Matthew 18:20

Grandchildren like to help. That's why you need a stool in your kitchen, so they can roll out pastry dough, push down on cookie cutters, and sprinkle sprinkles. Those youngsters are more than eager to stir paint, tighten a bolt, plant a pumpkin seed, or even change a tire. All you have to do is ask.

As a result, your grandchildren might learn about the consistency of paint, the universal rule of "righty tighty, lefty loosey," the miracle of growing giant gourds, or a skill that may come in real handy on a dark night on a dark road.

Parents don't always have time for such lessons. Typically, they are too busy doing the work to impart a lesson.

Similarly, you can teach even more important lessons by asking your grandchildren to do you another big favor. That is to pray for you.

Have you ever done that? Without even thinking too hard, you can probably come up with a dozen things going on in your life right now that could use some prayer. Your grandchildren might be the exact right recruits for that mission.

Frankly, the earnest prayer of a child with a pure and sincere heart sounds like an improvement over some of the pompous and pretentious prayers I hear from adults.

When making that request of your grandchildren, you'll want to choose the right issues to ask them to pray about. Don't put pressure on your young grandchildren to help make any adult decisions. Refrain from revealing secrets you don't want broadcast around the neighborhood or schoolyard. But do search your heart for a few legitimate prayer requests they can pray for you and with you.

Pray about new career or volunteer opportunities. Explain the pluses and minuses. Pray about whether you should get a new furnace, new roof, or new car, and how you want to be a faithful steward of your limited funds. Pray about a friend or colleague who is facing a life-threatening illness, marital crisis, or rebellious teenager. You don't have to give names or details. God knows all the details anyway. Pray for your aches and pains, but minimize any fears you may be putting into their little heads.

These prayers help kids realize they are not the center of the universe. It also helps them appreciate how good they have it. However, the biggest reason to pray with your grandkids is because prayer changes things. It moves God's heart. God heals. God opens doors. God brings clarity when we face difficult decisions. Your grandkids need to know how to plug into that power that hung the stars and gives us all life and breath.

WHAT ABOUT YOU?

We know that God always answers prayer. You can even make that promise to your grandchildren, but follow it up with a theologically correct explanation they can understand. God's answer will be yes, no, or not now. That may be oversimplified, but it's a place to start. Also, be clear that God has knowledge and plans that we can't possibly know. His ways are not our ways. (See Isaiah 55:8–9.) His answer to our prayer will be far better than what we can imagine. You can't go wrong explaining to your grandchildren, "We're not home yet. Someday God's answers will all be clear."

LONG-DISTANCE GRANDPARENTING

*For though I am absent from you in body, I am present with
you in spirit and delight to see how disciplined you are and how
firm your faith in Christ is.*
—Colossians 2:5

You moved to a warmer climate. Your son and his family moved out of
state to advance his career. Your daughter went to school out of state,
fell in love with a local boy, and never moved back home. Suddenly,
you're a long-distance grandparent.

Even worse, the "other" grandparents live near the kids, and you
feel left out. When you do get to see that growing family, you rush to
cram as much as you can into a few days. At your place, there's never
enough room. At their place, you feel like an intrusion. Motels are
impersonal—and expensive. However, your children and grandchildren need to feel your regular, consistent commitment and love. How
can you make that happen?

You need a plan to help turn the frustration of long-distance
grandparenting into a blessing.

First, communicate creatively via phone calls, e-mail, or text messages. One positive result of the COVID-19 pandemic is that Zoom
and other face-to-face digital options are now user-friendly and routine. Keep track of your grandkids' interests and schedules so that
your conversations can go deeper than "How's the weather?" Also,
the post office is still operational, and they could use your business.

Second, become a desirable destination point. Add kid-friendly
features to your home and yard. Research local events and destina-
tions. Open your home—for an extended visit—to one or two of
your grandkids at a time. If you can, offer to pay the airfare.

Third, realize that kids are busy, so don't panic if they can't always visit or talk. The last thing you want to do is add guilt or judgment to the communication you do have.

Fourth, trust God to provide a conduit for your love to flow easily over the miles. It's an opportunity to share and reflect God's love in your nearby community—to family, friends, and strangers. Too many long-distance grandparents focus on their loss, rather than on the gifts and opportunities they have. Make the most of this season that feels like a separation. When really it can be an opportunity for you to grow in your faith and build other relationships in new and exciting ways.

WHAT ABOUT YOU?

In the next few months—or the next few days—there will be opportunities for you to reach out and be an encouragement to one or more of your grandchildren, whether they live nearby or far away, in a manner you had not previously considered. But only if you look for it. Your only limit is your own imagination. Make it a quest. Make it fun. Make it a blessing.

WHEN I AM WEAK

*Some persons of weak understanding are so sensible of that
weakness, as to be able to make a good use of it.*
—François de La Rochefoucauld[4]

Have you thought about the wonderful way that 2 Corinthians 12:10 applies to grandparenting? Paul wrote, *"That is why, for Christ's sake, I delight in weaknesses, in insults, in hardships, in persecutions, in difficulties. For when I am weak, then I am strong."*

Over the years, most of us have tallied up decades' worth of weakness and distress. We've endured insults and hardships. Sometimes, as a result of simply standing up for our faith. What's more, those weaknesses seem to be coming faster and faster. Advancing age tends to do that.

In most cases, those weaknesses don't feel much like a gift. But what if you began to see them as an unmistakable delight? You may have missed it, but *"delight"* is a word Paul uses in 2 Corinthians 12:10. Can insults and hardship really be an opportunity for delight? Can weakness really be a conduit for personal strength? Does that sound impossible? Implausible?

Backing up just one verse in your Bible, Paul reminds us that grace is sufficient. Indeed, 2 Corinthians 12:9 confirms that Christ's power is *"made perfect in weakness"* and that we should *"boast all the more gladly"* about our weaknesses so that the power of Christ can work in and through us.

Still not buying it? A bit earlier in the passage, Paul describes how his own cryptic thorn in the flesh was initially a tormenting tool

---

4. François de La Rochefoucauld, *Maxims and Moral Reflections* (C. Whittingham, 1802), 1, https://archive.org/details/maximsmoralrefle00laro/page/n19/mode/2up.

of Satan. (See verse 7.) Three times Paul had pleaded to God for that pain to be taken away. In the end, Paul learns to embrace his torture—whatever it is—because he realizes that God is using it as a refining tool and a reminder that Jesus is enough.

Feeling your age and a bit of weakness? Spend a few minutes pondering the remarkable truths of 2 Corinthians, chapter 12.

WHAT ABOUT YOU?

In your role as a grandparent, how can you make use of—or even take delight in—your weaknesses? What positives might come out of those negatives? Consider any unexpected opportunities that might grow out of your recently acquired burdens and inabilities. For example, even though you can no longer climb trees, you can still identify birds, marvel at the autumn leaves, and applaud your grandson as he reaches new branches and new heights. Having forgotten the words to an old favorite hymn gives you the chance to discover them as if for the first time, along with your young granddaughter. Failing health or injury may find you asking a grandchild to shovel your sidewalk, program your entertainment system, retrieve a box of Christmas decorations, or push your wheelchair, giving them a chance to serve. That's a skill all young people need to practice and something in which you should readily find delight.

REMEMBER THE EMPTY NEST

Like arrows in the hands of a warrior
are children born in one's youth.
—Psalm 127:4

Before you became a grandparent, you may have gone through a season of life that had been eagerly awaited, not as easy as you thought, and brought its own share of second-guessing and worry. I'm referring to those bittersweet months or years of "the empty nest."

Every situation is different. But you may have had a hard time saying good-bye, letting go, cutting the cord, and wondering what the future would bring. Your home that was once so full of life, seemed almost desolate.

Somehow you survived the empty nest. What lessons did you learn that apply to your current role as grandparent?

You may have learned to embrace change and even replace fear or discomfort with a sense that a new calling, a new adventure awaits. Maybe God revealed to you a strategy for being bolder and seizing new opportunities as you claimed, for example, 2 Timothy 1:7: *"For the Spirit God gave us does not make us timid, but gives us power, love and self-discipline."* Power, love, and self-discipline are essential tools for facing any new season of life.

As grandparents, those skills will come in extra handy. On behalf of your adult children and their spouses, the goal is to maintain and even strengthen relationships. They may not say it out loud, but they still need you! When your kids ventured out on their own, they probably intentional about creating distance. They needed to prove they could make it. Now, as parents, they may have new questions and even some doubts. Don't be surprised if they begin to lean into a reinvented relationship with you.

Two words of caution: first, even as they seek your advice, don't expect the next generation of parents to agree with everything you suggest. Second, a renewed relationship with your adult children may come with some old baggage based on the eighteen-plus years they were under your care. Go ahead bring it up. You want to get to the point that together you can laugh at those days when you were both testing your boundaries.

Finally, just as your children left the nest a few years ago, even your youngest grandchildren will be doing the same thing sooner than you can imagine. As the years unfold, one of your goals is to help prepare them for their independence...while depending on the Lord.

WHAT ABOUT YOU?

Psalm 127:4 equates children with arrows. Well, arrows aren't achieving their purpose if they remain in the quiver. Grandparents and parents need to stand firm, sharpen each arrow, choose the right target, pull them close to your heart...and let them fly.

BUILD A LEGACY

*Then God blessed Noah and his sons, saying to them, "Be fruit-
ful and increase in number and fill the earth."*
—Genesis 9:1

A story I tell often in my talks to grandparents around the country
always gets me misty-eyed. The lead characters are my father and one
of my grandsons whom my father never got to meet.

To set the scene, you need to know that I had a solid relationship
with my dad. He was known as "Papa" to just about everyone, while I
am affectionately known as "Chief."

Here's how the story appears in my book *Hooray for Grandparents!*,
published a few years ago. Jackson, my grandson, is now in his teens!

My seven-year-old grandson was in our "upstairs playroom"
playing with the wooden Noah's Ark designed to fit our siz-
able collection of Beanie Babies. I realized it could be a nice
moment to connect Jackson with his great-grandfather who
had passed just two years before he was born. "Papa made
that," I told Jackson, "That's my dad."

Then, looking around the room, I realized we were surrounded by a wooden table, rocking elephant, Matchbox car
ramp, step stool, doll house, art easel, and Noah's Ark all
crafted with love by my father years ago for my own kids.

Overcome with emotions, I pointed out each of those handmade wooden creations to Jackson. With sudden determi-
nation, Jackson stood up and said, "Let's go, Chief. I need to
meet him!"

I gasped at the idea and the innocence of my grandson's request and I found myself overwhelmingly grateful for my father's legacy—one I had not previously fully recognized. I told my own grandson, "Well, Jackson, Papa's in heaven, and one day you will meet him. But isn't it great that part of him is still right here in all this stuff he made...and in me...and in you?"[5]

WHAT ABOUT YOU?

This story delivers a multitude of lessons.

First: if you're a carpenter, go ahead and use your skills to make toys and gifts that last for generations. A wooden Noah's Ark filled with Beanie Babies is an especially worthwhile project.

Second: tell your grandkids good stuff about your own parents and grandparents. For young people, there's value in knowing your heritage. As grandparents, we should be eager and intentional about sharing that legacy.

Third: spending one-on-one time with your grandchildren will inevitably open doors to spiritual conversations. Pray ahead of time for the right words to say.

5. Jay Payleitner, *Hooray for Grandparents!* (Chronicle Books, 2022), 140.

DAY 13

LEAN INTO THE GOOD

I praise you because I am fearfully and wonderfully made; your works are wonderful, I know that full well.
—Psalm 139:14

If you ask me, I'll tell you that my grandchildren are near perfect. What's more, I will confirm that my three sons and their wives are doing a fabulous job raising those kids.

Still, sometimes I'm not 100 percent sure about how my grandchildren are being instructed and disciplined. Of course, I haven't raised an eight-year-old in more than two decades, so I could be wrong. Times have changed. My memory gets fuzzy. Can you relate?

After they spend the day at your house, do your grandchildren leave a bit of a mess in the kitchen or family room? Have you noticed that the older siblings are a bit overbearing with the younger ones? Do those ungrateful young creatures sometimes leave the kitchen table after lunch without saying thank you or requesting to be excused? Do they splash in puddles, interrupt adult conversations, make up their own rules for games, pretend the sofa is a trampoline, laugh when someone farts, and ask "Why?" too often?

Terrible, isn't it? It would be easy to think the worst, blame their parents, and spend all day correcting their diabolical misbehavior. What to do? What to do?

Instead of dwelling on any perceived shortcomings, what if we chose to lean into the good? What if we saw those little rascals or older troublemakers as fearfully and wonderfully made? Once again, Scripture comes in quite handy when facing such a dilemma.

See grandkids as the gift they are.

"Children are a gift from the Lord; they are a reward from him." (Psalm 127:3 NLT)

Employ your grownup wisdom to give grace to parents and grandchildren.

"A person's wisdom yields patience; it is to one's glory to overlook an offense." (Proverbs 19:11)

Instead of being a grumpy old person, speak words of kindness, patience, and encouragement.

"Do not let any unwholesome talk come out of your mouths, but only what is helpful for building others up according to their needs, that it may benefit those who listen." (Ephesians 4:29)

See glimpses of God's nature and heart in your grandkids.

"So God created mankind in his own image, in the image of God he created them; male and female he created them." (Genesis 1:27)

The overarching point is to see your grandchildren through God's eyes. Maybe even more important, help them see themselves as beloved children of God, each created in His image, as a gift to your family and the world.

WHAT ABOUT YOU?

Can you lean into the good? Sure, there's a lot of frustration in the world and within your family. But don't lay that frustration on your young, impressionable grandchildren. After spending time with you, they should feel good about themselves. Even if you go a little overboard with your praise and encouragement, that's really okay. They may not get much of that anywhere else. In this season of life, elevating and encouraging grandchildren may be your primary job!

DAY 14

KEEP AN OPEN DOOR

But while he was still a long way off, his father saw him and
was filled with compassion for him; he ran to his son, threw his
arms around him and kissed him.
—Luke 15:20

My eldest son, Alec, and his wife, Lindsay, have a restaurant in the charming vacation town of Saugatuck in southwest Michigan. Every visit, I make sure to spend a few minutes in the quirky gift shops filled with knickknacks and wall plaques. I almost always find something that challenges me in my life or inspires my writing. Usually it's a clever turn of a phrase that's under ten words. Sometimes it's a paragraph. On my last visit, this sentiment was framed and for sale on the wall of one store:

> One day when my children are grown, I hope they will still come through the front door without knocking. I hope they head to the kitchen for a snack, and slump onto the sofa to watch TV. I hope they come in and feel the weight of adulthood leave them, for they are home. For my children, my door will forever be open.

I'm a bit embarrassed to confess that I didn't buy the piece. As much as I loved it, my wife, Rita, and I already have an abundance of readable art on our walls. These pieces include cross-stitched and calligraphed Scripture verses, Robert Frost poetry, and quotations about gardening, music, and child-rearing.

Still, the printed message at that gift shop resonated with me, as I hope it does with you. If we want to have any influence as grandparents, our own kids need to feel welcome and comfortable in our home. Yes, they should ask permission before they cut into the cake you made for guests arriving later. Yes, they need to move out before their thirtieth birthday. Yes, soon enough you can repurpose their old bedroom into a home office or prayer room. But they should always feel safe to come through your front door, be themselves, fill their bellies, and share with you the ups and downs of life.

If you still live in the home in which they grew up, their familiarity and sense of belonging should come easily. If you've downsized, that may be a little tougher, but the goal is the same. It's you who makes it inviting and comfy.

Remember also that the grandkids are watching. If there's tension in the air, they're the first to notice it. If harsh words are muttered (or shouted) by parents or grandparents, the children are often the ones most deeply affected. They feel it more intensely and carry the impact longer than anyone else in the room. Instead, put the past in the past and move forward into this new season. Even when you're Grandma and Grandpa, you'll still be Mom and Dad, and that's a good thing.

WHAT ABOUT YOU?

If you have a prodigal for whom you've been praying, this concept is even more important. Keep the light on and door unlocked. Scan the horizon routinely. When you see that wayward son or daughter a long way off, let compassion overflow, run to them, and deliver hugs and kisses without any hesitation.

LET THEM KNOW YOU NOTICE

When I was a child, I spoke and thought and reasoned as a child. But when I grew up, I put away childish things. Now we see things imperfectly, like puzzling reflections in a mirror, but then we will see everything with perfect clarity. All that I know now is partial and incomplete, but then I will know everything completely, just as God now knows me completely.
—1 Corinthians 13:11–12 (NLT)

Most grandparents don't see their grandchildren every day. If they live nearby, it might be once a week or so. If they live far away, they might see them only a few times a year. That gives you an advantage that their parents don't have. You notice the growth and, possibly, any new maturity. Moms and dads often miss it. Sometimes the emerging maturity of a grandson or granddaughter may even surprise you.

Next time that happens—especially if the grandkids are approaching those high school years—pull out your Bible and show them a verse that makes them feel like they're headed in the right direction.

Have them read 1 Corinthians 13:11–12 and then you might say something like this.

Can I say how much I appreciate the person you are becoming? Part of me doesn't want you to grow up too fast. But another part of me is really looking forward to seeing how you continue to use your gifts and talents. Like this verse says, you are "putting away childish things." I see you speaking and thinking in grown-up ways. It makes me smile when I imagine the future you have on earth. Plus, you have a future in heaven, which is impossible to imagine until we get there. I just want to say, "Keep at it!" And I want to remind you that God knows everything about you and will make sure you have everything you need.

Don't memorize that speech, but do read those verses with your young teenage grandchildren a few times and make sure they understand that you are watching and noticing. Let them know that, not long ago, they were little. They're growing up, and you love seeing the way God is working in their lives.

If it makes sense, extend the conversation by sharing your ideas about leadership, humility, self-discipline, dating, personal responsibility, clothing, money, homework, and goal setting. Young people want to think about themselves advancing in maturity. You can put a positive spin on who they are, what they can achieve, and how to give glory back to God.

Also, remind them there's no hurry to leave childhood behind, but emphasize that it's a joy to see them growing in maturity and grace. If it's your style, you can even joke that they're growing up too fast and demand they stay little for as long as possible.

WHAT ABOUT YOU?

On a personal level, grandparents should remember that anticipating the future on earth and in heaven is not just reserved for young people. With all you've learned from years of life experience and Bible study, you may have a clearer perspective of how God's plan works. Still, you should expect God to deliver some surprises for you along the way. Good luck with that!

REAL-LIFE EXPECTATIONS

Lower your expectations of earth.
This isn't heaven, so don't expect it to be.
—Max Lucado[6]

As grandparents, we often wonder about the best activities to do with our grandchildren. Sometimes, the uncertainty of what to do or how things will turn out holds us back. We certainly don't want to set out to bake cookies, build a birdhouse, or make a snowman and then fail miserably, do we? It would be a disaster if the cookies got burned, the access hole in the birdhouse was the wrong size, or the snow was not good for packing, right?

Well, actually, beginning a modest project with your grandchild and missing the mark completely can be a valuable learning experience. Young people need to know how to respond to failure because even the best plans can come up short. They need to know life goes on, and that, at least in most cases, you can try again. What's more, you've still made a memory! Hopefully it's something you can laugh at sooner or later.

The beauty of spending time with your grandchildren lies not in the perfection of the activity but in the shared experience. By stepping out in faith and simply beginning, you create opportunities to connect, experience joy, explore their gifts, and create something of lasting value.

On the other hand, there may be even greater value if Grandma and Grandpa are right there when the best-laid plans crash and burn.

---

6. "Heaven: God's Highest Hope," Words of Hope and Help, Max Lucado, accessed May 22, 2025, https://maxlucado.com/heaven-gods-highest-hope/.

Your grandchildren's parents put a certain level of expectations on their children. For the most part, that's a good thing. Moms and dads should encourage their kids to dream and set goals. That's how kids learn to put their best effort into worthwhile projects. Nevertheless, with expectations comes an occasional failure. When expectations aren't met, you can help your grandchildren know that it's not the end of the world.

Not to get too bleak, but depression among teens is on the rise. A recent study by the CDC found that 42 percent of high school students reported feeling so sad or hopeless almost every day for at least two weeks in a row that they stopped doing their usual activities.[7]

When your grandchildren fall short or completely fail at some new endeavor, you don't want them to feel despondent or without hope. Instead, take those opportunities to come alongside them and help them see that, as fallible humans, we are destined to make mistakes and come up short, but we have a loving God who never fails. Be ready to share with them Psalm 73:26: "*My flesh and my heart may fail, but God is the strength of my heart and my portion forever.*"

What a comfort that truth can be in the moment—and in the future, even when Grandma and Grandpa aren't around.

WHAT ABOUT YOU?

Over the decades, you have placed a wide range of standards on yourself and your family regarding career goals, financial security, exercise regimens, and all kinds of expectations shaped by cultural norms. Even now, you expect to see and hear from certain family members at regular intervals, right? Remembering that we're all human and offering a bit of grace may serve you well. But, most important, know that God is the true strength of your heart and your portion forever.

---

7. "Youth Risk Behavior Survey Data Summary & Trends Report," Youth Risk Behavior Surveillance System (YRBSS), Center for Disease Control (CDC), August 8, 2024, https://www.cdc.gov/healthyyouth/data/yrbs/pdf/YRBS_Data-Summary-Trends_Report2023_508.pdf, page 60.

DAY 17

PRAY WHAT MATTERS

When you ask, you do not receive, because you ask with wrong motives, that you may spend what you get on your pleasures.
—James 4:3

I know you pray for your grandchildren. But what are you praying for? That your grandson or granddaughter makes the basketball team? That they find a date for the prom? That they get into a certain prestigious university? That their acne clears up?

Well, go for it. Pray for those things.

Are you surprised by that recommendation? It's really okay. God wants you to come before Him with your whole heart. Plus, you do want your grandchildren to find a measure of joy and satisfaction in life.

What's more, I'm on record saying that we should never judge prayer. Short prayers. Long prayers. Boring prayers. Prayers for things we don't really need. Prayers that may seem redundant. God hears them all, and He answers them, often in unexpected ways.

Still, it's always wise to consider your motives when you pray. Do you want your grandchildren to have success in life in order to bring glory to God, or so you can brag to your friends? Are you praying from your own flawed earthly perspective or for God's will?

Ground your prayer in Colossians 3:1–2: *"Since, then, you have been raised with Christ, set your hearts on things above, where Christ is, seated at the right hand of God. Set your minds on things above, not on earthly things."*

A truly surrendered prayer might sound something like this: "God, pull my grandkids close to You." In many ways, that says it all.

But here's a slightly longer version that I hope reflects your deepest desire for those young ones you love so much.

> Heavenly Father, please draw my precious grandchildren close to You. Help them make morally sound choices. Help them discover their gifts and use those gifts to give You glory. When they fail or make mistakes, help them know that You are a God of second chances. Help them feel Your unconditional love, seek forgiveness, and make things right. Reveal to them the sin in their lives and help them fully understand their need for a Savior to take the penalty for that sin. Help them accept Your gift of grace at an early age. Introduce them to people in their lives who are positive role models—people who know and follow You. I pray also, Lord, for their future spouses. Protect the hearts of those boys and girls whom they may not have even met yet! And, Lord, help me be the kind of grandparent You want me to be. Thank You for such an amazing privilege. In Jesus's name, amen.

WHAT ABOUT YOU?

Even if you are tight with your adult children and their families, you can't always know what's going on in their heads. The temptations. The fears. The daily difficult decisions. It's impossible for you to know the opportunities and dangers around the next corner. God knows, and He's waiting for your prayers.

SPRINKLING STARDUST

Nobody can do for little children what grandparents do.
Grandparents sort of sprinkle stardust over
the lives of little children.
—Alex Haley [8]

Today's devotion comes with a recommendation and a challenge.

When your grandkids are little—say, age two to about seven years old—feel free to lean into the goofiness of youth. Let Mom and Dad be the disciplinarians. Grandma and Grandpa should be mostly purveyors of treats and cheerleaders, representing the joy of life. Your rallying cry could be, "Joie de vivre."

From preschool to the age of accountability, children have an innocence that needs to be cultivated, even rewarded. Imagine anything that might bring joy to a typical first grader. Tickling. Blowing bubbles. Building a fort with couch cushions and blankets. Knock-knock jokes. Sidewalk chalk. Burbling tummies. Lying in the grass watching clouds. Building and destroying block towers. Catching frogs or fireflies. Playing "I Spy." Puppets. Hide-and-seek. Tea parties. Dancing in the kitchen. Chucking rocks in a pond. And so on.

Last weekend, four-year-old Finn and I took a break from his sister's soccer game and walked across the park to the jungle gym. On the way, the sun was at our backs, creating long shadows in front of us. I firmly warned Finn not to step on my shadow. Of course he did. I dodged and weaved. Finn gleefully jumped and stomped. So silly it was. As silly as sprinkling stardust.

---

8. Statement in Reader's Digest (1987), as quoted in Marilyn R. Zuckerman and Lewis J. Hatala, *Incredibly American: Releasing the Heart of Quality* (Milwaukee, WI: 1992), 13.

My recommendation, then, is to find joy in the goofiness of youth when they are not yet accountable for their moral choices. A pre-schooler or child in early grammar school can be taught right from wrong, but they may not have the capacity to know why. However, they can experience and understand joy. That season of life provides the optimum chance for them to learn how to give and receive joy, along with a reminder of the Inventor and ultimate Source of joy.

As a matter of fact, grandparents who orchestrate moments of joy have the right and responsibility to make the connection and give gratitude to God for whatever is bringing their grandchild joy in the moment. Not as a lecture, but as a prayer of gratitude in the moment.

Which brings us, as promised, to that challenge. Grandparents, one of your missions should be to continue cultivating joy beyond those early years and into the lives of your pre-teen, teenage, and young adult grandchildren. If you don't, who will?

You might even pray Romans 15:13 right out loud before, during, or after a joy-filled activity: *"May the God of hope fill you with all joy and peace as you trust in him, so that you may overflow with hope by the power of the Holy Spirit."*

You could paraphrase that verse, but it's such a wonderful blessing, it's worth memorizing and voicing word for word.

WHAT ABOUT YOU?

Do you have the courage and foresight to help your growing grandchildren link trusting God and experiencing the power of the Holy Spirit with activities like blowing bubbles, dancing in the kitchen, snowboarding, axe throwing, making milkshakes, picking wildflowers, picking apples, and stomping on shadows as you walk to the jungle gym? Can you see the connection?

READ THE LOCAL PAPER

Live such good lives among the pagans that, though they accuse
you of doing wrong, they may see your good deeds and glorify
God on the day he visits us.
—1 Peter 2:12

In discussions with my children after my father passed away, I learned something about the power of an involved grandparent. It turns out that he's still teaching me lessons I can use.

My dad was the principal of a local elementary school for over thirty years, and he knew many names of former students in the community. During his years as a grandfather, "Papa" also read the local paper every morning. Every once in a while—not too often—he'd come across a name he recognized in the police report. It was usually in association with a minor crime that tended to show up in small-town newspapers: public intoxication, reckless driving, vandalism, shoplifting, petty theft, and so forth.

What I didn't know until later was that Papa had a little routine whenever he spotted one of his former students in the paper. Casually, almost offhandedly, he'd mention to his grandchildren that so-and-so had been fined or picked up by the police. Sometimes that was the end of it. On other occasions, he'd offer a sideways warning, with a look that said more than his words. He'd say something like, "That's a real shame. I know that family, and I'm sure their parents are plenty embarrassed by all this. I expect the only time I'll see the Payleitner name in the paper is on the sports page, or maybe for some award or recognition for a job well done."

Unbeknownst to me, he had that kind of conversation over the years with all our kids. What's more, my five grown children confirmed that through their teenage years, they thought about Papa's words often. None of them was destined for a life of crime, but they were well aware that the reputation of our family mattered. Since our last name wasn't Smith or Johnson, everyone in town knew all the Payleitners were related. When that name showed up in print, it would come with either a dose of pride or a tinge of shame.

The good news is that Alec, Randall, Max, Isaac, and Rae Anne all did get their names in the paper on a few occasions—and, indeed, it was always good news.

Please don't think I'm bragging. I only intend to confirm that every family has a reputation, and it starts with past generations and continues down the line. Proverbs 22:1 confirms, "*A good name is more desirable than great riches; to be esteemed is better than silver or gold.*"

The overarching lesson from my dad might be that we should find ways to share hopes, dreams, warnings, and even expectations with our grandchildren without making our words sound like a threat or command.

WHAT ABOUT YOU?

Of course, we shouldn't live our lives seeking to please others above all else. The apostle Paul put it this way: "*Am I now trying to win the approval of human beings, or of God? Or am I trying to please people? If I were still trying to please people, I would not be a servant of Christ*" (Galatians 1:10).

However, much of our witness really does depend on others observing us and our families and thinking, "I want what they have."

EXPLAIN SYZYGY

When I consider your heavens, the work of your fingers,
the moon and the stars, which you have set in place,
hat is mankind that you are mindful of them,
human beings that you care for them?
—Psalm 8:3–4

Your grandkids are curious. They actually like learning stuff on their own terms. While they may not always like the stuff they are forced to learn at school, they are almost always on board when a grandparent treats a walk in the woods or an evening stargazing event as a wondrous series of discoveries.

The key is for you to be a trusted truth-telling expert while uncovering uncharted territories. Maybe you've done (or will do) some of these activities:

Lying on the grass with a four-year-old and following the path of a ladybug. A few years later, spinning a globe and sharing the surprising serpentine curve of the Isthmus of Panama connecting North America with South America. Taking them to a ball game and teaching them how to fill out a scorecard. Explaining yeast fermentation while watching a loaf of bread rise through the glass door of your oven. Pondering the many ways that God designed plants to spread their seeds—cockleburs caught on socks, dandelion puffs, squirrels burying nuts, coconuts floating to the next island, or birds eating berries and pooping out seeds a mile away.

For their first decade or so, you can be the wise dispenser of all this knowledge. As they get older, there are fewer and fewer things you'll know that they don't. So, to help keep you one step ahead, it's time to teach you something so you can teach it to them. I'm 99 percent sure your teenager does not know the very cool-looking word *syzygy*.

Syzygy (pronounced SIH-zih-jee) is the scientific term for the alignment of three celestial bodies.[9] The most obvious examples are solar and lunar eclipses. Now, listen carefully; there will be a test.

A *solar* eclipse is when the moon sneaks between the earth and the sun, blocking out some or most of the sun's rays for a short period of time. A solar eclipse happens during the day, and if it's a total eclipse, it will bring virtual darkness to its path, which may stretch as wide as seventy miles.

A *lunar* eclipse is when the earth passes between the sun and the moon, casting an obvious shadow on the surface of the moon. Please don't confuse the relatively rare lunar eclipse with the monthly lunar cycle during which you see new moons, quarter moons, half-moons, and full moons.

An online search will reveal more about the where, when, and how of syzygies and eclipses.

Sharing new discoveries with your kids—especially about Creation—is really just a sneaky way to open the door to conversations about the Creator. The more your grandchildren know about the wonder of nature, the more they will appreciate the glory of God.

WHAT ABOUT YOU?

Of course, you don't have to teach the meaning of syzygy to your grandkids. But you do have to engage them in ways beyond asking, "How's school?" and "Are you hungry?"

---

9. *Merriam-Webster.com Dictionary*, s.v. "syzygy," accessed May 22, 2025, https://www.merriam-webster.com/dictionary/syzygy.

RESPONDING TO BUSYNESS

Too much activity gives you restless dreams;
too many words make you a fool.
—Ecclesiastes 5:3 (NLT)

Are your grandkids going a million miles per hour? That's not unusual. Our culture feeds into a fast-paced lifestyle.

Almost all growing families today seem to have jam-packed schedules and regularly race across town from one activity to the other. That includes every sport imaginable requiring team practices and individual lessons. Plus, kids are getting involved earlier and earlier in artistic, dramatic, and musical pursuits.

It's not unusual for kids—starting as young as four years old—to have close to a dozen can't-miss events on their schedule each week. Lessons in everything from archery to zither are happening after school, early evening, after dinner, and all day Saturday. Unfortunately, in many communities, Sunday mornings and Wednesday evenings are no longer set aside for church activities.

Moms and dads text and delegate, jockeying their own schedules around their children's activities. For dinner, they pick up fast food for fast lives. To say the least, life is full.

I know what you're thinking. But really, fully engaged lives are probably okay. Maybe even a good thing. Children today might have a better chance at uncovering their personal giftedness, not to mention learning to keep a schedule, meet deadlines, and adapt to change.

It's certainly better than vegging out in front of a television. Also, they never really get bored or permanently discouraged. If one activity is frustrating or ends with tears, they don't have to wait long until another activity comes along, giving them another chance for success.

If this describes your grandkids, you may be wondering how you fit in and what role you should expect to play.

First, be an encourager and even a cheerleader. It would be really easy—and not surprising—if Gram or Gramps felt the urge to express a negative opinion of their kids' frenetic lifestyle. Please don't. Casting aspersions on choices made by your son or daughter will not end well.

Second, if possible, see if you can ease some of the stress. If you find yourself being an extra driver, watching a toddler, shooting videos, or filling in the gaps in some other way, that's not being an enabler. That's supporting your family in their time of need.

Third, as part of their support system, you will have earned the right to offer a suggestion or two about their schedule. Especially when it comes to prioritizing church and faith-building activities for the kids.

WHAT ABOUT YOU?

If you're there for the whirlwind of activity, there's a good chance you'll also be there for moments of calm. That's when you can take a few minutes between activities to tell the story of Mary and Martha from Luke 10:38–42. When Jesus came to the home of the two sisters, Martha busied herself trying to make everything perfect for their guest, only to become worried and upset. Mary made a better choice, sitting quietly at the Lord's feet and listening to what He said.

DAY 22

CONSOLATION AND SALVATION

This is my comfort in my affliction,
that your promise gives me life.
—Psalm 119:50 (ESV)

Over the decades, most grandparents will have spent some time in the hospital. Maybe it was a visit to the ER, which is never a quick trip. Or perhaps injuries from an accident required a long season of rehab and recovery. More than a few grandparents have endured extensive surgery, difficulty having some mysterious illness diagnosed, weeks or months of intensive chemotherapy, or a scheduled joint replacement. Beyond the birth of a healthy child, most hospital visits are not experiences we want to dwell on.

The entire misadventure of being poked and prodded is never easy, and you may still have some lingering symptoms or discomfort. You want to forget all that, don't you?

Honestly, you shouldn't.

This may sound paradoxical to most people, but for those who have been following Christ for a while, it really won't be surprising. Friend, there's purpose in your pain. Purpose beyond your imagination. Ask yourself, in your suffering: did you find comfort in God? Did your dire circumstances here in this world give you an appreciation for the transformed body you'll be receiving in the next? That's the underlying message of this passage from 2 Corinthians:

Praise be to the God and Father of our Lord Jesus Christ, the
Father of compassion and the God of all comfort, who comforts
us in all our troubles, so that we can comfort those in any trouble
with the comfort we ourselves receive from God. For just as we

share abundantly in the sufferings of Christ, so also our comfort abounds through Christ. If we are distressed, it is for your comfort and salvation; if we are comforted, it is for your comfort, which produces in you patient endurance of the same sufferings we suffer. And our hope for you is firm, because we know that just as you share in our sufferings, so also you share in our comfort. (2 Corinthians 1:3–7)

In this passage, Paul is referring to any and all afflictions and challenges of life, not limited to physical trauma. No matter what trouble we may endure, Paul makes it clear that even as we receive Christ's comfort, we need to look for opportunities to pass that comfort on to others.

In the weeks and years following our suffering, we should expect opportunities to share in the suffering of others, opening the door for us to also share comfort.

WHAT ABOUT YOU?

Grandparents, I pray that you and your loved ones will not endure long battles with illness, injury, and physical distress. But Jesus has said that in this world, there will be troubles. (See John 16:33.) The God of comfort wants to use you—and everything you've gone through—to minister to your children, grandchildren, and anyone you know who needs a ray of hope during a crisis. What an honor to be used by God in that way!

DAY 23

IT'S YOUR TIME

Teach us to number our days,
that we may gain a heart of wisdom.
—Psalm 90:12

There's something—perhaps way in the back of your head—that you've wanted to do for a long time. Instead, life had other plans.

You're not filled with regrets. Raising a family is no small obligation, and you wisely chose to invest much of your time, brainpower, resources, and emotional energy into that worthwhile endeavor. Along the way, you often put the needs of others before your own—especially in times of crisis and uncertainty.

You made sacrifices. That's what parents do. Even if they don't say it, your children and grandchildren appreciate your selflessness. Still, your unspoken dream lingers. Have you forgotten it? Or is it still there? Maybe even still reachable?

This season of life called grandparenting often comes with an entirely new set of obligations. Count heads and you'll discover you're actually directly responsible for fewer people than when you were parenting. For some grandparents, it might be just you and your spouse. Or just you! Sure, your adult children occasionally need your wisdom and help, and you can always choose to make yourself available in a pinch. But, really, these next decades could be your time to shine—maybe even in a surprising new way.

While you read the preceding paragraphs, one specific activity or dream may have sprung to mind. You know what? Go for it. Do some research. Pray. Google those three or four words and see if they open new doors in your life.

If nothing comes to mind, here are a few ideas that may help you recall some dream set aside decades ago. Open a diner. Get a poem published. Write your memoirs. Buy a pottery wheel. Do a short-term mission trip. Learn a foreign language. Become a foster parent. Go to seminary. Circle the globe. Get your CDL, LPN, EMT, or CPA. Take up golf, tennis, cycling, swimming, curling, or pickleball. Train for a marathon. Add to a collection you've already started. Learn to play the piano or guitar. Buy a drum kit. Join the local drama group or the worship team at church. Run for office. Get your degree. Prepare to earn your pilot's license. The sky's the limit.

What does this have to do with your role as a grandparent? For your grandkids' sake, one of your goals is to stay interesting. Instead of being an old fuddy-duddy who talks only about the weather and your aches and pains, your conversations could be filled with stories of your own new experiences, which opens the door for them to tell you about theirs!

Perhaps even more important is the idea that your grown children need to know that Mom and Dad have their own life and schedule. While you will eagerly make time for watching the grandkids and scheduling vacations and outings, they shouldn't assume that you're waiting around with nothing to do.

WHAT ABOUT YOU?

Benjamin Franklin is credited with having said, "You may delay, but time will not." And that's worth remembering. One year from now, you either will have gained a year's experience in something worthwhile, or you will still be deciding whether or not to take a leap of faith. In both cases twelve months will have gone by. Which means you can either spend the next year pursuing your dream, learning from mistakes, and getting ready for your second year of exploring life anew; or, you can be waiting for someone else to take the glory. Glory you could have earned and given to God.

YOUR GREATEST FEAR

You are as much serving God in looking after
your own children, and training them up in God's fear, minding
the house, and making your household a church for God, as you
would be if you had been called to
lead an army to battle for the Lord of Hosts.
—Charles Spurgeon[10]

In my travels speaking to grandparents—especially in church settings—there's one single issue that causes concern above and beyond any other. I suspect that apprehension is top of mind among many of the grandparents who picked up this devotional.

For sure, grandparents may fret about their grandchildren regarding education, health, mental health, safety, screen time, relationships, and commitment to family. You also want to know how to make the most of the time you have with them. Specifically, how to have fun with those kids you love so much and occasionally sneak in a lesson on values and what's really important in life. Those are all valid grandparenting ruminations.

However, time and again, the greatest fear I hear from grandparents is the uncertainty of whether their grandchildren will be joining them in heaven.

That is a reasonable fear. Grandparents are acutely aware of what's happening, both globally and in the lives of their grandchildren. Young people—even those who seemingly walked with Christ for years—are falling away from the church. When you were raising

---

10. Charles Spurgeon, *Strengthening Medicine for God's Servants*, accessed June 9, 2025, https://www.spurgeon.org/resource-library/sermons/strengthening-medicine-for-gods-servants/#flipbook/.

your own children, you learned that being a Christian parent requires more than simply going through the motions. You can't just check a few boxes and expect your kids to recognize their need for a Savior, make a genuine personal decision for Christ, and pursue a lifelong relationship with Him.

In many cases, you sent your kids to Sunday school, Bible camp, AWANA, Royal Rangers, Pioneer Clubs, VBS, Young Life, and youth group; you encouraged them to get involved in young adult activities at your local church or campus. You prayed for them. You had heart-to-heart conversations with them about God's love and the truth of the Bible. After they grew up and moved out of town, you asked carefully worded questions like, "Hey, have you found a good church in Charlotte?" or "What do your weekends look like in Fort Collins?"

Now, when they come visit you on a weekend, they may or may not join you in your old pew on Sunday morning. You're also afraid to talk about faith because you enjoy their company, and you don't want to offend. It's heartbreaking, but you find yourself wondering if you could have done more and how this impacts the next generation.

What is your role in the ongoing faith development—and the very salvation—of your adult children and their children? Let's explore that question in the next two devotions.

WHAT ABOUT YOU?

Are you secure in your salvation? If not, please take care of that neglected essential ASAP.

DAY 25
YOUR OWN CHILDREN

Tell it to your children, and let your children tell it to their children, and their children to the next generation.
—Joel 1:3

Here's how faith sharing in families is supposed to work. Each generation has a responsibility to pass the family history down to its own children. That includes frustrations and breakthroughs, family traditions, lessons learned, repentance proclaimed, and blessings received. All in preparation for the day of the Lord, when God will bring judgment on all humankind.

That's the overarching message of the prophet Joel. The Old Testament book named after him takes up just a few pages in your Bible, and it's worth a fresh read. The description of the plague of locusts (which reflects the sinful nature of our world) is a bit frightening, but for those who respond to God's call to repentance, this is the promise: *"I will repay you for the years the locusts have eaten"* (Joel 2:25).

How does Joel imagine the way all that restoration will take place? He describes how generational connections empowered by the Holy Spirit will lead to visions. Sons and daughters, old and young, will inspire people everywhere to call on the name of the Lord and be saved.

> *I will pour out my Spirit on all people. Your sons and daughters will prophesy, your old men will dream dreams, your young men will see visions.... I will show wonders in the heavens and on the earth, blood and fire and billows of smoke. The sun will be turned to darkness and the moon to blood before the coming of the great and dreadful day of the LORD. And everyone who calls on the name of the LORD will be saved.* (Joel 2:28, 30–32)

Please don't miss this: the opening paragraph of the book of Joel explains that believers are supposed to *"tell it to their children"* (Joel 1:3). Each generation is responsible for speaking into the lives of the next.

I know what you're thinking. Have I done my job as a parent? Are my own children on the right track? Have they ever heard and accepted the complete gospel? Even if they made a decision for Christ in their younger days, did they understand what they were saying? These are not easy questions.

Ask most pastors, and they'll try to be encouraging and optimistic. But the honest answer can be found in Romans 14:12: *"Each of us will give an account of ourselves to God."* Keep praying and recognize that God looks at the heart, the Holy Spirit is still at work, and Jesus died for the whole world.

WHAT ABOUT YOU?

Have you experienced locusts sweeping through your life? That's part of your story. Plus, you're not alone. Others—including members of your family—need to hear how God rescued you, restored you, and repaid you for the years the locusts have eaten.

MODELING FAITH TO YOUR GRANDCHILDREN

We will not hide them from their descendants; we will tell the next generation the praiseworthy deeds of the LORD, his power, and the wonders he has done.
—Psalm 78:4

Let's get right to it. For several reasons, it's not easy to preach the gospel to your grandchildren. A long list of challenges comes to mind. Pushback from Mom and Dad. Limited time. Hesitation that they'll push you away. Fear of using the wrong words. Fear of rejection because you think you only have one shot at it. Feelings of unworthiness because of your own shortcomings and not wanting to seem hypocritical. Afraid they'll ask questions you can't answer.

None of that matters.

First, take to heart Deuteronomy 4:9: *"Only be careful, and watch yourselves closely so that you do not forget the things your eyes have seen or let them fade from your heart as long as you live. Teach them to your children and to their children after them."*

In other words, you've seen stuff and know stuff your kids' kids need to know. Your knowledge and experiences should be passed down to the next generations. Children need proof that salvation is worth the effort and that God is worthy of our devotion. They need to hear personal stories of how an authentic Christian faith makes a real difference in a real person's life. Grandma and Gramps, you're nominated.

Second, celebrate the doubts and questions of your grandchildren. That's right! Having authentic faith requires overcoming some doubt.

Never forget the reason Jesus spoke the life-changing words of John 14:6: "*I am the way, the truth, and the life. No one can come to the Father except through me*" (NLT). He was responding to the wonderful, honest confusion of our old friend Doubting Thomas, who asked, "*Lord, we don't know where you are going, so how can we know the way?*" (John 14:5).

Third, bear fruit in your own life. As Jesus said, "*I am the vine; you are the branches. If you remain in me and I in you, you will bear much fruit; apart from me you can do nothing*" (John 15:5). Stay connected to God, and your grandkids will notice your love, generosity, peace, kindness, and winsomeness. At some point, they'll want what you have.

Which leads to point four. "*Always be prepared to give an answer to everyone who asks you to give the reason for the hope that you have. But do this with gentleness and respect*" (1 Peter 3:15). Because you're so awesome, your grandkids will eventually ask, "Why?" Tell them it's because you have Jesus in your life.

Again, give the Holy Spirit some room to work. Share your story. Expect their doubts. Bear fruit. Expect God to create an opening to share with your loved ones the source of the hope you have.

WHAT ABOUT YOU?

Any impact you're going to have on your grandchildren's faith requires you first to have a mutually loving relationship with them. So please remember to love first. Actually, that's solid advice anytime you hope to present the gospel to anyone. Love first.

DAY 27

PASSING THE CROWN

Children's children are a crown to the aged,
and parents are the pride of their children.
—Proverbs 17:6

Does your family have any cherished keepsakes or heirlooms passed down from generation to generation? Maybe Great-Grandma's engagement ring was used by several men in succession when proposing to their future bride. Significant sentimental value may be attached to a pocket watch, cradle, heirloom hunting rifle, vintage model train, grandfather clock, classic Gibson guitar, or hand-carved nativity set. A handmade quilt or embroidered linen could be more than a century old. Many families hand down a leatherbound Bible inscribed with handwritten genealogies. To my sons, I have passed on woodworking tools used by my grandfather.

The market value of such items may not be significant, but they're not really for sale anyway.

A popular notion indicates upcoming generations are not exactly eager to inherit Grandma's hutch or that trunk full of photos and letters. Gen Xers and millennials pride themselves on living without clutter. They move more often and don't have room for such treasures. Words, music, and images are stored digitally. They shudder when they consider the gargantuan task of helping their parents and grandparents—that's you—clean out attics and basements.

All of which brings us to the metaphorical crown mentioned in Proverbs 17:6. Please don't miss the opportunity to cherish that crown and lovingly pass it on. This crown is all about the honor and joy grandchildren bring to their grandparents. The verse also calls us to reflect on the value of this relationship. That crown is not just a decoration; it symbolizes a legacy, something precious to your generation and those that follow.

Keep reading that verse, and you come to a clear instruction: Parents should make their children proud. Is that true in your family? Are your grandchildren proud of their mom and dad? I hope so. Strong families are built on the younger generation respecting and looking up to their parents. That's how wisdom is passed on.

The obvious next question relevant to anyone reading this devotional is this: Have you earned and maintained the respect of your own grown children? Are they proud of you?

WHAT ABOUT YOU?

You may be insulted when your kids or grandkids don't get excited about inheriting a piece of furniture, fine china, antiques, photo albums, tools, or other heirlooms that you have been saving for them. If that emotion hits you hard, take a moment to think about what's really important. What do you most want to pass on to the upcoming generations? Search your heart and you'll discover that respect is the crown you want as your legacy. To make your children proud, take note of this instruction from Titus 2:7–8: *"Show yourself in all respects to be a model of good works, and in your teaching show integrity, dignity, and sound speech that cannot be condemned"* (ESV).

PLANT SEEDS

So neither the one who plants nor the one who waters is anything, but only God, who makes things grow.
—1 Corinthians 3:7

This spring—whether you live on a farm, keep a backyard garden, or simply have a sunny windowsill—invite your grandchildren to plant some easy-to-grow seeds and monitor their progress over the growing season. Then anticipate opportunities to deliver all kinds of lessons.

You could buy starter plants, but I recommend starting with good soil and planting seeds at just the right depth. That's when you want to have a casual conversation about the importance of cultivating a heart receptive to God's Word and the value of being surrounded by a community filled with love and support. You could share this verse as you do:

But the seed falling on good soil refers to someone who hears the word and understands it. This is the one who produces a crop, yielding a hundred, sixty or thirty times what was sown.
(Matthew 13:23)

When the grandkids check a few days later, they may be frustrated by the lack of any sprouts. Give it a few more days, and you'll have a surefire biblical object lesson in patience.

Let us not become weary in doing good, for at the proper time we will reap a harvest if we do not give up. (Galatians 6:9)

When the grandkids come over and marvel at how big your plants have grown, talk about how small acts of faith and obedience can have a big impact.

He told them another parable: "The kingdom of heaven is like a mustard seed, which a man took and planted in his field. Though it is the smallest of all seeds, yet when it grows, it is the largest of garden plants and becomes a tree, so that the birds come and perch in its branches."   (Matthew 13:31–32)

Finish up by giving all the glory to God. You and your grandchildren can take credit for the *idea* to plant a garden. You even prepared the soil, planted the seed, watered, fertilized, and harvested. But confirm that none of that happens without the Creator of the universe.

So neither the one who plants nor the one who waters is anything, but only God, who makes things grow.

(1 Corinthians 3:7)

WHAT ABOUT YOU?

One of the remarkable spiritual rewards of having grandchildren is that you begin to see the world through their eyes. Over the years, simple truths you learned long ago may be forgotten or taken for granted. Our life experience has led to a certain level of cynicism, jadedness, and world-weariness. As part of God's design for grandparents, time with grandkids just might wash away some of that junk to reveal a new path of appreciation for God's sovereignty and the restoration and renewal of our faith.

WHATEVER?

Gray hair is a crown of splendor;
it is attained in the way of righteousness.
—Proverbs 16:31

Okay, so you can't do a cartwheel anymore. Tree climbing, cliff diving, and swing dancing are not on your schedule this week. You also can't remember the name of the dog owned by your best friend from high school. You misplaced your car keys this morning. Really, it's okay.

You may have lost some physical dexterity, and your memory may need a reboot; but, with age and experience, you've gained so much more.

Think about everything God has taught you while on the job, raising your family, and engaging with friends and neighbors. You've learned through trial and error, and just staying aware of the amazing world around you. By the time you become a grandparent, you already had a good sense of what is true, noble, pure, and admirable. By the time you reached grandparenting age, your own elders and dearest friends were modeling priorities and pursuits that have brought God's peace into your life.

Programming our minds in this way is a theme of the last chapter of Paul's letter to the church at Philippi. The entire letter is filled with joy and gratitude, but it's Philippians 4:8–9 that calls us to a heavenly frame of mind.

Finally, brothers and sisters, whatever is true, whatever is noble, whatever is right, whatever is pure, whatever is lovely, whatever is admirable—if anything is excellent or praiseworthy—think about such things. Whatever you have learned or received or heard from me, or seen in me—put it into practice. And the God of peace will be with you.

Too many people can look around and completely overlook anything that is lovely, noble, or admirable. We close our minds and become set in our ways. We look at the same walls, the same screens, the same desktop. We get lazy, complacent, or cynical. Somehow, we can even look at a breathtaking sunset, an intricate spiderweb, or the radiant face of a young grandchild, and fail to see the wonder of creation.

Seeing beauty and pointing it out to our grandchildren is one of the great privileges of grandparenthood. I urge you to notice whatever is true, whatever is pure, and whatever is lovely. Whatever you have learned in your fifty-plus years of life, consider it a gift from God and allow it to inspire you to action. Go wherever it takes you. Bring your grandson or granddaughter along for the ride. Whatever you do, don't miss it.

The result? The God of peace will be with you.

WHAT ABOUT YOU?

It happens a lot. People who can no longer do cartwheels or frequently lose their car keys think the best of life is over. As a result, they close themselves off from the world, go on cruise control, or start listing regrets and broken dreams. If they're lucky, a grandchild or two comes into their life and stirs things up. Suddenly, they stop shrugging their shoulders at life with a sarcastic and monotone, "Whatever." Instead, they remember what God has taught them over the years and say, "Whatever You need, Lord. I'm here. Use me!"

EMBRACE A CHILDLIKE FAITH

The soul is healed by being with children.
—Fyodor Dostoevsky[11]

Too often, we grandparents think we're smarter than the rest of the family. And why not? We've done more, seen more, and made more mistakes. We know what works and what doesn't.

As enlightened adults, we employ our advanced education, common sense, and deductive reasoning to explain...well, everything. However, if we're honest, we're forced to admit there are still many concepts mere humans can never fully understand, such as how the universe began, why bad things happen to good people, how all dogs go to heaven, if streets in heaven are really paved with gold, how Noah kept the lions from eating the zebras, how many licks it takes to get to the center of a Tootsie Roll Pop, and so on.

Deep thinkers may claim to have answers, but there needs to be room for uncertainty. The Bible clearly states heaven cannot be described: *"No eye has seen, no ear has heard, and no mind has imagined what God has prepared for those who love him"* (1 Corinthians 2:9 NLT).

What's more, authentic Christians readily accept our limited earthly perspective. *"Now we see things imperfectly, like puzzling reflections in a mirror, but then we will see everything with perfect clarity"* (1 Corinthians 13:12 NLT).

Before society shifted toward moral relativism, the belief that the human mind simply couldn't comprehend heaven or God's perspective was embraced by people of faith. The idea was cherished.

---

11. Fyodor Dostoevsky, *The Idiot* (William Heinemann, 1913), 65, https://books. google.com/books?id=JYNLAQAAMAAJ&q=%22is+healed%22#v=snippet &q=%22is%20healed%22&f=false.

However, today's culture of so-called enlightenment labels such faith as ignorance and even uses "living by faith" to argue against the existence of God.

Faced with this dilemma, authentic Christians would do well to step back from claiming to have all the answers and instead embrace a childlike faith—curious, wide-eyed, dependent, and trusting. I believe that's what Jesus meant when He said, "*Truly I tell you, unless you change and become like little children, you will never enter the kingdom of heaven*" (Matthew 18:3).

When Bible scholars consider the issue of childlike faith, they agree. It's not being childish or ignorant or naive. Childlike faith means you finally see God as a trustworthy heavenly Father on whom you can depend.

As we mature in Christ, 1 Corinthians 13:11 applies: "*When I was a child, I talked like a child, I thought like a child, I reasoned like a child. When I became a man, I put the ways of childhood behind me.*" The ability to reason like a mature adult can be a satisfying season. We need to be thinking Christians.

Once in a while, when we're tired or beaten up, or when doubt creeps in, we shouldn't hesitate to come back to our heavenly Father and say, "Let me rest in You."

WHAT ABOUT YOU?

Unfortunately, since humans really can't conceive of heaven, some choose not to believe at all. That may include our sons, daughters, grandchildren, and others we love so much. In response to their skepticism, our most effective role is not as the authoritative, all-knowing truth teller. The best strategy for engaging those with whom we want to have a long-lasting, trusting relationship is to be childlike and acknowledge God as being beyond human understanding. We might even come alongside our family members in their quest for what really matters. Empathize with their healthy skepticism. Perhaps even say something like, "Isn't it great that God has a plan beyond our comprehension? I'm glad He's in charge and not me!"

MISSION DRIFT

*We must pay the most careful attention, therefore, to what we
have heard, so that we do not drift away.*
—Hebrews 2:1

An individual or organization is said to experience "mission drift"
when it sets forth on a noble cause but then, for some reason, deviates
from the original purpose. For example, the YMCA was founded in
1844 to promote Bible study and Christian values among young men.
Harvard University, founded in 1636, was established to train clergy
for Christian ministry. Often, nonprofit organizations are launched
with the best of intentions, only to be derailed by greed, mismanage-
ment, or a dubious social agenda.

Successful family businesses might succumb to mission drift
when the visionary founder passes the company on to the next generation, who grew up watching Dad work long hours and make sacrifices but lacks his fire and ambition. That second generation may
manage to keep the company afloat while enjoying the fruits of the
old man's labor. Almost inevitably, when the founder's grandchildren
take over the reins, they take wealth for granted and take all kinds of
liberties including driving expensive cars while driving the company
into the ground. It's a classic American story, and yet the long-re-
tired or deceased founder somehow gets blamed for the failure of the
company.

Another version of mission drift can occur in families when it
comes to authentic and active faith in Jesus and the mission to live
and share the gospel.

In the life of any believer, there's a moment of revelation when
they understand and accept the sacrificial love of Jesus as expressed

on the cross. That personal moment of justification triggers a range of instant benefits, including a clean slate from all sin, a hunger to know more about Jesus and the Bible, indwelling by the Holy Spirit, an awareness that everything that happens in life can be used for good, and the guarantee of eternal life in heaven.

In essence, new believers gain a new mission that impacts their motivations and choices for the rest of their lives. Yet, the timing may be such that their children never see the difference Jesus makes. Without appreciating the before and after, that next generation will never see how Jesus changes everything.

When that happens—unless the story is told—generational drift begins. Children of first-generation believers have less passion, are more easily distracted, tend toward pushback, and fail to see the immediate and long-term benefits of the Christian life. Subsequently, the grandkids almost don't have a chance.

Here are a couple of questions for grandparents to ponder: Who represents the first generation of authentic believers in your family? How can you prevent mission drift for your kids and their kids?

WHAT ABOUT YOU?

The takeaway might be to make sure the next generations know your redemption story. If you hit bottom, talk about how God rescued you.

> I waited patiently for the LORD; he turned to me and heard my cry. He lifted me out of the slimy pit, out of the mud and mire; he set my feet on a rock and gave me a firm place to stand. He put a new song in my mouth, a hymn of praise to our God. Many will see and fear the LORD and put their trust in him.
>
> (Psalm 40:1–3)

Be a living testimony to the value of crying out to the Lord and leaving the slimy pit behind me. Your grandchildren—especially teenagers—will soak in your story of brokenness and redemption.

FIND THE SMILE

I thank my God every time I remember you. In all my prayers
for all of you, I always pray with joy.
—Philippians 1:3–4

Here's an exercise that will take your thoughts and prayers for your grandchildren and translate them into joy—and, sometimes, action.

Choose one grandkid at a time and simply think about them until you smile. Think about their eyes, hugs, laughs, frowny faces, and thoughtful faces. Imagine their future. Imagine the next time you get to see them.

If you've chosen a four-year-old grandson or granddaughter, it's easy. Your smile will come quickly. At that age, kids tend to be surprising, energy-filled goofballs that say very silly and sometimes very profound things.

Newborns also promote instant smiling. That's because they are all potential. The future has no limits. As they absorb the sights and sounds of the world, you can tell they are learning something every moment. Babies and toddlers learn more in one day than you have learned in the last six months. Right?

Middle schoolers are also going through moments of self-discovery. Plus, moments of rejection, frustration, and confusion. That's the middle school experience. With that understanding, smile because you know there's light at the end of the tunnel.

Thinking about older teens or young adults may leave you scratching your head. They are facing decisions you never even considered. Technology and culture have come so far. Still, you should be able to consider their heart, mind, and soul and find reason to smile.

Or maybe this exercise is difficult. Some grandparents may even be angry reading this devotional. They have grandchildren they don't know or can't know. Perhaps a grandchild has become a burden on the entire family because of some bad decisions. You may feel helpless, but you are not! You're still here. They're still here. What if you reached out and entered their life in a whole new way? Imagine you and them on a park bench, taking a road trip, or seeking out the right doctor, social worker, or spiritual leader. Many young people just need someone who loves them to be the wind beneath their wings. This may be your most important calling ever.

Finally, maybe you cannot smile because one of your grandkids has left this world, and you don't want to think about the pain of that loss. But, as a grandparent, that's another gift you can bring to your family. Be the one who is not afraid—at the right time—to remember that precious life and express love and appreciation for what they meant to so many people.

This grandparenting exercise is a private endeavor. But the result is hope, appreciation, and joy that can overflow onto the entire family. Discovering or rediscovering your smile is a chance to clear away some of the darkness and fog, so you can envision a bright future for those young people you love so much.[12]

WHAT ABOUT YOU?

In your quest for smiles as you imagine your grandchildren, accept this prayer from the apostle Paul in the book of Romans: *"May the God of hope fill you with all joy and peace as you trust in him, so that you may overflow with hope by the power of the Holy Spirit"* (Romans 15:13).

---

12. Adapted from Jay Payleitner, *Hooray for Grandparents!* (Chronicle Books, 2022), 195–198.

BE A STORYTELLER

*Jesus spoke all these things to the crowd in parables; he did not
say anything to them without using a parable.
So was fulfilled what was spoken through the prophet:
"I will open my mouth in parables, I will utter things hidden
since the creation of the world."*
—Matthew 13:34–35

In your ongoing quest to be like Jesus, you have been given a tool that uniquely qualifies you to impact the lives of your grandchildren in major ways. Better than anyone else, you can tell stories!

Your storytelling arsenal is unlimited. You have stories from your own youth, from when your own children were young and foolish, and stories from Mother Goose and Dr. Seuss. You know stories from history books…and history you've witnessed firsthand. Best of all, you know, stories from the Bible.

The key to your storytelling is to end with a nugget of wisdom. You already know that if you start with a lesson, your grandkids will tune out. Yet, if you start with a good story, they're hooked. Matthew 13:34–35 reminds us that Jesus spoke in parables, thus fulfilling prophecy.

Psalm 78 is especially relevant to grandparents because it emphasizes the value of passing along lessons learned the hard way to future generations.

*My people, hear my teaching; listen to the words of my mouth.
I will open my mouth with a parable; I will utter hidden things,
things from of old—things we have heard and known, things
our ancestors have told us. We will not hide them from their*

descendants; we will tell the next generation the praiseworthy deeds of the Lord, *his power, and the wonders he has done. He decreed statutes for Jacob and established the law in Israel, which he commanded our ancestors to teach their children, so the next generation would know them, even the children yet to be born, and they in turn would tell their children. Then they would put their trust in God and would not forget his deeds but would keep his commands. They would not be like their ancestors—a stubborn and rebellious generation, whose hearts were not loyal to God, whose spirits were not faithful to him.* (Psalm 78:1–8)

So, Grammy and Gramps, don't hide things from of old. Tell the next generation the Lord's praiseworthy deeds. Make sure they know the law and put their trust in God. Maybe even take advantage of any of your grandchildren's stubborn and rebellious moments as a reason to turn to the Psalms and say, "Hey, young rebel, your stubbornness is nothing new. And, by the way, your actions and attitude may lead to consequences you may regret."

WHAT ABOUT YOU?

Psalm 78 goes on for seventy-two verses. After reading the passage above a few times, open your own Bible to read that entire psalm, which includes a complete review of the plagues of Egypt, the original Passover, and a reminder that God should not be put to the test. Mercifully, the passage ends with the Lord choosing the tribe of Judah and appointing David to shepherd the people with integrity of heart.

BE A GRAND FRIEND

A friend loves at all times.
—Proverbs 17:17

Friendship is a unique bond that brings joy, comfort, and understanding. While parents often have the challenging role of setting boundaries and guiding their children through life's ups and downs, grandparents have the opportunity to form a different kind of relationship. You can be that special friend who knows all about your grandchildren and loves them unconditionally.

Parents are tasked with the difficult work of discipline and instruction, creating a dynamic where friendship might not always be appropriate or possible. They need to maintain authority and provide structure, which can sometimes create friction. But, as a grandparent, you have a better chance to offer a safe haven of friendship where your grandchildren feel accepted and cherished.

Think about the qualities of a good friend—someone who listens without judgment, provides support, and shares in joys and sorrows. These are the same qualities you can bring into your relationship with your grandchildren. By being their friend, you provide a different perspective and a valuable complement to their parents' roles.

Here are some ways to cultivate a friendship with your grandchildren:

- **Practice Active Listening:** Take time to really listen to your grandchildren. Ask about their day, their thoughts, and their feelings. Show genuine interest in their lives and validate their experiences.

+ **Pursue Shared Activities:** Find common interests you can enjoy together. Whether it's playing games, cooking, gardening, or even just watching a favorite show, shared moments build a bond of friendship.

+ **Prioritize Open Communication:** Let your grandchildren know they can talk to you about anything. Create a safe space for them to express themselves without fear of judgment. Maybe even share secrets!

+ **Praise Accomplishments and Celebrate Milestones:** Be their biggest cheerleader. Others may forget, but grandparents always, always remember to acknowledge achievements and milestones. And anniversaries of milestones. Your presence and encouragement mean more than you know.

+ **Provide Wisdom:** Build trust by strategically delivering insight that grandkids can use that comes across as supportive rather than instructive. Instead of saying, "Do this," try saying, "What if…?" That's the mark of a true friend.

+ **Receive Their Friendship:** Allow them to teach, serve, celebrate, and support you. Help them see their value and realize that to gain friends, you have to be a friend.

WHAT ABOUT YOU?

Today, reach out to your grandchildren and spend quality time with them in a way that fosters friendship. Whether it's a phone call, a visit, or a shared activity, let them know you are there for them, not just as a grandparent but also as a friend. Embrace the opportunity to be the person who knows all about them and loves them unconditionally. You'll create a lasting bond that will enrich both your lives— long after you're gone.

DAY 35
NO REGRETS

A man is not old until regrets take the place of dreams.
—John Barrymore[13]

Growing old is a journey filled with both joy and apprehension. As grandparents, we cherish every moment with our grandchildren, marveling at their growth and the unique individuals they are becoming. Yet, alongside the joy, there can be a lingering fear—fear of growing old and the inevitable day when we may no longer be physically present in their lives. We think, "Will they miss us? Will they even remember us? Have we done all we could to leave our legacy? How can I best use the time I have left with these young people I love so dearly and worry so much about?"

You shouldn't be surprised to discover that Scripture offers us comfort, perspective, and instruction. Psalm 71:18 provides a valuable outlook that comes in the form of a prayer: *"Even when I am old and gray, do not forsake me, my God, till I declare your power to the next generation, your mighty acts to all who are to come."*

There's a lot of subtext to that psalm. Read it a couple of times, then let's dig into it.

First, most of the men and women reading this devotional are either in or entering the season of being old and gray, but that's not something we should assume. Some folks never make it to our age. So our first response should be gratitude.

Second, the Bible tells us over and over that God will not abandon or disown believers, so why does the psalmist fret that God will *"forsake me"*? That worry has no place in our hearts or minds.

---

13. Gene Fowler, *Good Night, Sweet Prince* (Viking Press, 1943), 178.

Third, the psalmist understands that we've been given an imme-diate assignment: to *"declare [God's] power to the next generation."* But for some reason, we're in procrastination mode. We're asking for more time, when really we should be actively fulfilling that assignment.

Fourth, the psalm even includes a strategy for making that dec-laration. It's not just saying, "God is powerful"; it's all about looking back at your own life, recognizing God's *"mighty acts,"* and then relat-ing them to your grandchildren. In other words, telling your story.

Finally, remember that Psalm 71:18 is a heartfelt prayer. Recite it often and you'll see any anxiety or regret wash away. Here it is one more time: *"Even when I am old and gray, do not forsake me, my God, till I declare your power to the next generation, your mighty acts to all who are to come."*

WHAT ABOUT YOU?

Initially, Psalm 71:18 acknowledges that it's not unusual to be a little anxious regarding what God has planned for this season of life. Becoming old and gray naturally leads to questions like, "What's next?" Thankfully, we're then given an immediate assignment. That is to declare God's power to our children and their children. Are you up to the task? What will it take?

READING HEZEKIAH

Each generation tells of your faithfulness to the next.
—Isaiah 38:19 (NLT)

There's an old joke about a pastor who opened his sermon asking his congregation for a show of hands from anyone who had recently "read through the book of Hezekiah." Without hesitation, about half the attendees—not wanting to look unspiritual—raised their hand.

Well, of course, there is no book of Hezekiah. However, that king of Judah did have a profound impact on Israel, and his story shows up in 2 Kings, 2 Chronicles, and Isaiah. He became known as a reformer and literally cleaned house, removing pagan shrines and idols, even "[breaking] *into pieces the bronze snake Moses had made, for up to that time the Israelites had been burning incense to it*" (2 Kings 18:4).

Even though he was a proud man, Hezekiah found favor with God. When a prophet revealed he had a terminal illness, Hezekiah lifted a sincere prayer and wept bitterly. After being granted an additional fifteen years of life, he wrote a lengthy emotional poem acknowledging his mortality, offering gratitude for his healing, and promising to use his additional time to praise God and speak of His faithfulness.

Specifically, Hezekiah singles out the impact that parents—while they are alive—can have on the next generation. *"Only the living can praise you as I do today. Each generation tells of your faithfulness to the next"* (Isaiah 38:19 NLT).

History reveals that King Hezekiah may not have taken his own advice. His own son, Manasseh, desecrated Solomon's temple with idols, worshipped pagan gods, and even sacrificed his own children to idols.

It isn't difficult to make the connection between killing children to honor idols and today's ongoing scourge of abortion. It also seems fitting to ask how Hezekiah could have influenced his son to stop the massacre. In the same way, as generational leaders of our families, what should be our response to the million or more children aborted each year?

There's more to the story of Hezekiah, but the lessons for parents and grandparents today are profound. Ask yourself, "Does my life give praise to God? What idols am I worshipping?" It may not be bronze snakes, but, over the course of a month, you can probably identify a few earthly or evil distractions that have turned your attention from our Creator God.

Finally, perhaps we shouldn't be so hard on Hezekiah for the sins of his son, Manasseh. Parents are surely responsible for doing their best in leading their children to a life of faith, but each individual is ultimately responsible for their own choices. *"So then, each of us will give an account of ourselves to God"* (Romans 14:12).

WHAT ABOUT YOU?

According to the mandate in Isaiah 38, the responsibility to tell the next generation about God's faithfulness seems to fall on the parents. Did you follow through on that assignment with your own children? If God gave you fifteen years—starting today—how would you use that time to reach your children and your children's children?

PRAYABLE MOMENTS

Rejoice always, pray continually, give thanks in all
circumstances; for this is God's will for you in Christ Jesus.
—1 Thessalonians 5:16–18

Your words are powerful tools when it comes to sharing your faith with your grandchildren. But much more effective than preaching at them is praying with them.

When you pray with your grandkids—or even when they overhear you pray—you are modeling so much. You're demonstrating your belief in a loving God who answers prayer. You're illustrating how to pray sincerely, humbly, and expectantly. You're placing your trust in the One who made you. Depending on what you're praying for, you're displaying empathy, compassion, gratitude, resilience, community, and faith.

I recommend you be proactive about praying with your grandchildren. Think of it as simply being aware of "prayable moments."

Examples?

+ You and your little grandson or granddaughter are doing chalk pictures on the sidewalk, and you hear a siren several blocks away. Stop and pray. You don't know the details of that emergency, but God does.

+ You're stuck in a slight traffic jam on the way to school, church, a concert, or a sporting event. Turn off the car radio and pray that—no matter when you get there—God be honored in the upcoming event.

+ A storm front is moving in. Pray for the safety of your family and your neighbors.

+ You pass a church where wedding guests are throwing rice at a bride and groom, or you pass a car with a "Just Married" sign on the back. That's a fun, prayable moment. Offer a prayer for those newlyweds and add a prayer of thanks for your own spouse and for your grandchildren's mom and dad.

+ Through social media, radio, TV, or another outlet, you find out about a breaking national or international news event. Whether it's good news or bad news, stop for a moment with your grandchildren and express thanks to God that He is in control.

When you experience a need or see God working, you very likely offer a quiet prayer of supplication or thanksgiving. But—other than prayers before a meal or at bedtime—you probably don't involve your grandkids. One of the great benefits of prayable moments is how it gives them a view of the world beyond themselves. You're helping them become thoughtful, caring, and praying adults.[14]

WHAT ABOUT YOU?

You might already be aware of teachable moments. For example, grocery shopping, walking in the woods, or playing board games with your grandkids provides a wide range of teachable moments about picking ripe watermelons, protecting wildlife habitats, and playing fair and square. But taking advantage of prayable moments with your grandchildren will help them see the world through the eyes of God.

---

14. Excerpted in part from Jay Payleitner, *52 Things to Pray for Your Kids* (Harvest House, 2015), 15–17.

MUTUAL RENEWAL

Therefore, I urge you, brothers and sisters, in view of God's mercy, to offer your bodies as a living sacrifice, holy and pleasing to God—this is your true and proper worship. Do not conform to the pattern of this world, but be transformed by the renewing of your mind. Then you will be able to test and approve what God's will is—his good, pleasing and perfect will.
—Romans 12:1–2

We expect the question "What is God's will for my life?" to perplex and even frustrate young believers. They have so many choices. They are torn between living for the moment and making decisions that will impact their entire future. Adding to the confusion, adults in their lives offer contradictory input: "Let kids be kids" and "You know, the stupid things you do today will follow you the rest of your life."

Then—with the best of intentions—most kids growing up have been told, "You can be anything you want to be." That can put a lot of pressure on a young teenager.

If we're honest with ourselves, we'll admit that we are still asking ourselves that same question. What *is* God's will for my life? Really, that's a good thing. At any and every age, we *need* to be in constant pursuit of how God wants us to live.

Which brings us to this idea. What if—at the appropriate time—you let your grandchild know that you are going through a season during which you are wondering about what's next in your own life?

Would that blow their mind? Would they think, "If an old person doesn't know God's plan, how could I ever be sure of mine?"

Or would they be cool with it? Would they even begin to appreciate that this life is a journey and seeking God's will is part of the adventure?

If you're ready for it, this could be the beginning of a long conversation and journey of self-discovery for both of you. One approach would be to put the question out there and promise to share discoveries with each other over the course of several weeks. Along the way, open your Bible to reveal a "new insight" from the opening verses of Romans 12. Ask that teenage grandchild, "How can our bodies be a living sacrifice?" "How can that be worship...I thought singing was worship?" and "Do you think the test described in this verse will really work?" Confess that in your past, you made the mistake of conforming *"to the pattern of* [the] *world."* Depending on the maturity of your grandchild, you may even describe how that didn't work out so well. Assure them that God was using that time to draw you ever closer to Himself. Maybe He was even preparing you for your role as a grandparent!

Remember to do as much listening as possible. Remember also to expect God to reveal legitimate guidance to your grandchild. And to you!

WHAT ABOUT YOU?

You may think this is some clever way to get grandkids to open the Bible and think about God. And it is! More than that, it's also demonstrating that walking with God is a lifelong pursuit. Our life on this planet is a constant quest to renew our minds, giving us the ability *"to test and approve what God's will is—His good, pleasing and perfect will."*

BELIEVE MIGHTY ACTS

One generation commends your works to another;
they tell of your mighty acts.
—Psalm 145:4

How has God intervened in your life? The very fact that you're reading this devotional suggests that God has touched your heart and mind, guided you through some life challenges, and met your needs along the way.

You might not have had a near-death experience that gave you a glimpse of heaven and wound up as a story told in a best-selling memoir or blockbuster movie. You may not have seen an angel, survived a natural disaster, or been healed from a terminal illness. Yet, God has most certainly cleared a path, revealed a truth, or given you a sudden burst of clarity regarding a critical life decision.

It's true that sometimes Christians call something a miracle that is really just a coincidence or a close call that went your way. The one time I was ill-prepared for a college exam, was it a miracle when my professor didn't show up for class that day? Probably not. When a windstorm blew down the tree in our side yard, it didn't fall on my fence or my house. I'm glad about that, but I wouldn't call it a miracle.

However, I can point to close to a dozen experiences over the years that I would call miracles. You might not think of them as mighty acts, but I do.

An unexpected check in the mail for the exact amount of an unexpected bill. The attendant at the Michigan Visitor Center, who recovered my stolen wallet just ten seconds after I prayed about it. The perfect family showing up to adopt our toddler foster son, and I mean perfect. Getting fired from my job at a big Chicago advertising agency and stumbling into a life-changing job in Christian media and radio production.

Those are some of the miracles—life stories in which I can clearly see God's intervention—that I share eagerly with friends, in books, and from pulpits. As my eight grandkids get older, I promise to continue sharing these *"mighty acts"* with each of them.

God uses miracles. He always has and still does. I hope you tell your own grandchildren about miracles recorded in your Bible and newsworthy miracles about rescued miners, plane crash survivors, or a child recovered after a week in the wilderness. But because they know and love you, real-life true stories from Grandma and Grandpa carry significantly more impact.

WHAT ABOUT YOU?

Don't you dare suggest that you've never experienced any mighty acts of God. You may not have realized it at the time, but He has opened doors, spared you from catastrophe, steered you from a bad decision, calmed you with His peace in a high-stress situation, and performed other minor miracles that are worth remembering, cherishing, and sharing.

HEROES WATCHING

True heroism is remarkably sober, very undramatic.
It is not the urge to surpass all others at whatever cost,
but the urge to serve others at whatever cost.
—Arthur Ashe[15]

Grandparents, you are being watched.

Your grandchildren run through the front door, eager to see your smiling face and outstretched arms. In some cases, they never know what to expect from Gammy and Poppa. Sometimes you're all joy and delight. Sometimes you're a little tired or grouchy. Always remember how easily their little hearts can be wounded.

Your adult kids also still need your example, and they are watching to see how you fit into their lives. Can they count on you to help with the kids? Are you going to say or do something that contradicts their own parenting choices? How's your health? How's your driving? When will they need to take your car keys? You spent two decades looking out for them. Be glad they're looking out for you.

Others outside your family are also watching. Any new Christians you may know are eager to see if their new faith works for the long haul. Grandparenting peers are looking for someone they can trust and befriend, like-minded seniors who still have a zest for life and vision for the future.

What's more, there is another crowd whose eyes are watching you: past heroes of the faith. The book of Hebrews describes how they cheer us to a strong finish. Hebrews 12:1–2 reads, "*Therefore,*

---

15. Mary Meyer, "Ashe 'Set Standard for Human Beings,'" *The Delaware Gazette*, February 8, 2993, https://www.newspapers.com/image/882047842/?match=1&terms=arthur%20ashe.

since we have so great a cloud of witnesses surrounding us, let us also lay aside every encumbrance and the sin which so easily entangles us, and let us run with endurance the race that is set before us, fixing our eyes on Jesus" (NASB1995).

You may think this compelling verse is about perseverance—and you wouldn't be wrong. However, it's also about running a predetermined racecourse *"set before us"* and seeing our clear goal by *"fixing our eyes on Jesus."* The deeper meaning of this passage from Hebrews might be that equally as important as endurance is identifying the right goal chosen by God for each one of us and knowing who is waiting at the finish line.

We certainly don't want to finish our earthly race and suddenly realize that we've been running the wrong route.

WHAT ABOUT YOU?

The heroes of the faith described in Hebrews chapter 11 include Abel, Noah, Abraham, Isaac, Moses, Rahab, David, Samuel, and the prophets. Make sure you point out these role models to your grandchildren. Those young people you love so much need their example as well as your example. Do whatever it takes to help them feel inspired, encouraged, and applauded by you and those iconic biblical figures.

BUYING THEIR LOVE

For the love of money is a root of all kinds of evil. Some people,
eager for money, have wandered from the faith and pierced
themselves with many griefs.
—1 Timothy 6:10

Quite a few grandparents will occasionally slip a silver dollar or a five-spot to a grandchild. In some families, it's a longstanding tradition. (Though, with inflation, the value of those bills might need a little adjusting!) Personally, I think the practice is perfectly fine. A token financial gift falls in the same grey area as taking a grandchild out for ice cream. It's not special treatment; it's just part of the adventure of the day.

Still, be careful and don't get carried away. Being too generous can put you on thin ice with other members of the family. Especially if it seems like you're playing favorites.

Big fat checks and bills of larger denominations should probably be saved for special occasions. Who can argue with the wonderful tradition of getting a significant monetary congratulations from grandparents in honor of a first communion, confirmation, college graduation, or marriage?

Well, hold on, now. Here's something that may not have occurred to you. What about that grandchild who drops out of school to go into the trades or military? What about the one grandchild who chooses not to get married? Should we really be paying young people for spiritual milestones?

It's tempting for grandparents to use financial gifts as a sort of bribery to advance an agenda. Just don't overlook the possible repercussions. Know that it doesn't take much—just a few dollars here or there—to cause dissension among all those young people that mean so much to you.

Another challenge surfaces when financial rewards are based on performance. Ten dollars for A's on report cards. Fifty dollars for reading a book. Two hundred dollars if you come for an afternoon visit. A thousand dollars for quitting smoking. Those are all good things for your grandkids to do. What about the grandchild who gets B's in much more challenging college prep classes? Or lives too far away to visit? Or has dyslexia? Or never smoked to begin with?

Grandparents really do need to think this through. There's a good chance some of your grandkids are already feeling left behind or out of the loop. It's natural to reward grandchildren when they get applause and accolades for their successes. However, it's worth the effort to avoid making siblings and cousins envious in the process.[16]

WHAT ABOUT YOU?

Money should not be equated with love, but it often is! Without realizing it, you may be teaching your grandchildren that money equates to happiness. You know the first part of 1 Timothy 6:10. But the entire verse is worth rereading and taking to heart, especially realizing that your actions and attitudes speak more clearly than any verbal lessons.

---

16. Adapted from Payleitner, *Hooray for Grandparents!* 109–111.

GOTTA LOVE GREASY SPOONS

Remember the days of old; consider the generations long past.
Ask your father and he will tell you, your elders,
and they will explain to you.
—Deuteronomy 32:7

Bible scholars will tell you that this verse, written by Moses near the end of his life, exhorts the people to never forget what the Lord has done for them—including delivering them from slavery in Egypt, providing for them in the wilderness, and even establishing the twelve tribes of Israel generations before.

Applied today, that same verse is a challenge to grandparents to make sure future generations know how God continues to be faithful in good times and bad. That includes telling your grandchildren how God watched over you through your own long-ago challenges of youth: winless seasons of peewee basketball, an algebra teacher who put you to sleep, having to wear ill-fitting hand-me-downs, haircuts by your mom, group science projects with the classroom slacker, taking your cousin to a school dance, a first job for below minimum wage, and a crush on your speech teacher.

Relating these lessons requires sitting together in a place that evokes memories and prompts stories. What better place than a greasy spoon that serves dishes just like Great-Grandma used to make on plates older than your grandkids?

Here's the point. When moms and dads need to feed the family on the road, they look for a sure thing. That means any trip with your grandkids to McDonald's, Cracker Barrel, Denny's, Red Robin, Applebee's, Olive Garden, or IHOP will be uninspiring. There's nothing wrong with those chain restaurants. They're safe and predictable.

But may I suggest that safety and predictability are not the reasons children go out to eat with Grandma and Grandpa?

Your grandkids will remember the place where the jukebox played only Dolly Parton or the special of the day was pickled pig's snout. They'll marvel at the spinning pastries. Forever they will quote the waitress who stuck her pencil up in her babushka, called your grandson "Sweetie pie," and yelled your entire order in greasy-spoon slang to Festus the short-order cook.

They'll remember the life lessons you shared in those red vinyl-upholstered booths.

Be warned. Your stop at that vintage diner may completely backfire. Bad coffee. Burnt toast. Mushy veggies. Sticky floors. Nasty servers. Nasty restrooms. And spoons that are a little too greasy. Nonetheless, that's still a grandparenting victory, yielding one more example of how you and they can survive anything.

WHAT ABOUT YOU?

Giving your grandchildren a taste of vintage America is never a waste. That includes introducing them to soda fountains, roller rinks, historic motels, five-and-dime stores, boardwalk amusements, and drive-in movies. For good measure, also invite them to go with you to a tiny small-town church that still has a belfry, pipe organ, and fiery preacher talking about hell and damnation. Expect more good conversation after.

WHAT SUSTAINS YOU?

Old age may have its limitations and challenges,
but in spite of them, our latter years can be some of the most
rewarding and fulfilling of our lives.
—Billy Graham[17]

What keeps you going? What motivates you? I'm guessing that, at one point in your life, it was the almighty dollar. Even if you completely understand that money can't buy you love and *"the love of money is a root of all kinds of evil"* (1 Timothy 6:10), seeking more money to buy more stuff is a common human weakness.

For a season, perhaps you were motivated by attention from the opposite sex. That's also part of the human DNA. God did call us to be fruitful and multiply. (See Genesis 1:28.) However, we're also told to keep the marriage bed pure. (See Hebrews 13:4.)

Many older adults can look back and see seasons marked by an obsession with working out, status and power, self-expression, intellectual growth, social justice, environmental activism, fashion trends, aggressive beauty regimens, travel, adventure, or creating a fabulous and enviable online persona.

These are not all bad things. In reasonable measures, these endeavors deliver much to pursue and enjoy. Yet, in the end, you already know that such obsessions or inclinations will leave you empty. More money, firmer abs, more likes, and steamier romance will not sustain you. Worldly obsessions don't last or bring contentment.

Then what does sustain, satisfy, and rescue us from a life without meaning?

---

17. Billy Graham, *Nearing Home: Life, Faith, and Finishing Well* (Thomas Nelson, 2011), 24.

The answer won't surprise you. What might surprise you is how a pointed and resolute promise from a beloved Old Testament prophet is not directed toward immature young people who desperately need wisdom and direction in their lives. Isaiah 46:4 promises that God will sustain, satisfy, and rescue folks like you and me: *"Even to your old age and gray hairs I am he, I am he who will sustain you. I have made you and I will carry you; I will sustain you and I will rescue you."*

The prophet Isaiah leads up to this promise by documenting how pagan gods and carved idols need to be hauled around on the backs of mules. By contrast, the God of Israel has proven time and again that He does the heavy lifting. He is a God like no other. From the beginning, He has demonstrated how He carries, sustains, and rescues His people. That provision will continue through our future, collective and individual—even when we are old and gray.

Notice that God doesn't promise to eliminate challenges and adversities. No matter what your age, God will sustain you! When you need a lift, God will carry you! When you are broken, neglected, or even on the edge of a cliff, God will rescue you!

WHAT ABOUT YOU?

What a confidence builder this is for grandparents. What a witness that is to the next generation. Surrender to God and lean into His faithfulness. In His graciousness, He will empower your role as patriarch and matriarch of your family. When used to build the kingdom of God, He might even foster a few of your worldly capabilities and possessions. Keep your focus on Him, and He may even bless and sustain your aspirations and passions, using them in ministry and for the strengthening of human relationships. Whether it's improved health, a little adventure, intellectual stimulation, or some other enjoyable pastime, don't be surprised if God sustains you—as promised—to be a continuing inspiration and enjoyable companion with those grandchildren you love so much.

OBJECT LESSONS

*The Advocate, the Holy Spirit, whom the Father will send
in my name, will teach you all things and will remind you of
everything I have said to you.*
—John 14:26

Several times a month, you come across a spiritual lesson you want to teach your grandkids. I know that because I do the same thing. It might be a simple truth I heard from a preacher or a podcast. It might be an object lesson that triggered a breakthrough moment in my own spiritual journey. Or maybe it's something I tried to teach my own kids back in the day.

Examples of kid-friendly spiritual lessons are easy to find online. Here are a few worth trying.

On a nature walk, pick a three-leaf clover to help describe the Trinity. Chase a butterfly while relating the metamorphosis of a caterpillar in a chrysalis to the process of being born again.

At Christmas, pass out candy canes and relate their shape to a shepherd's crook. Explain that the hard candy represents Jesus the Rock, and the red stripes depict the blood He shed for us.

Play a whispering game that prompts your grandkids to walk closer and closer to each other, then explain James 4:8, which promises, *"Come near to God and he will come near to you."*

Shake a can of soda and talk about the explosive power of holding on to sinful anger. Put a five-pound hand weight in their backpack to help them understand the burden of not forgiving their enemy. Burst some bubbles or balloons to make the point that earthly things don't last.

Ideas like this sound fun and doable, so why don't we take advantage of them? It's not because we're lazy or don't care. It might be that we don't know how to start. We don't want to get the metaphor or analogy wrong. We certainly don't want our grandkids to be bored or think we're just being silly. We also don't want to get the theology wrong. Or maybe we're just too busy.

Here's something we all need to remember (myself included!): God will honor our efforts. When we're intentional about sharing spiritual lessons with our grandkids, God is right in the middle of that process. We may be planting seeds or opening doors for future conversations. The entire effort might be simply confirming to those kids that our faith is important to us.

Finally, don't forget to give the Holy Spirit a little room to work. Be intentional, creative, and diligent, but remember that our human limitations confirm our need for supernatural intervention. Romans 8:26 tells us, *"The Spirit helps us in our weakness."*

If you're still not sure where to start, I recommend the book *The Very Best, Hands-On, Kinda Dangerous Family Devotions* by Tim Shoemaker.

WHAT ABOUT YOU?

Remember that we never really know when a single, simple truth penetrates a child's mind and heart. A silly activity or lesson we initiate might be life-changing for any child at any age. We may not know the importance of that impact for many years. Indeed, as grandparents, we may not know until we step over that threshold into eternity.

GENERATIONAL CURSE?

"The past is never dead. It's not even past."
—William Faulkner[18]

One of the toughest things about being a grandparent is watching *your* children make mistakes with *their* children. Especially when you recognize that many of their worst parenting traits were picked up from you. Did you scream about spilled milk? Did you make promises but not follow through? Did you too often prioritize your career, hobbies, or other distractions over your family?

First, stop feeling guilty. In our sinful condition, we all make mistakes. The Bible confirms over and over that God is compassionate and that His grace covers our sins.

Still, you may have read passages in Scripture that describe the possibility of a "generational curse." Reflecting on your sinful past, Deuteronomy 5:9 may have left you especially concerned about your legacy: *"I, the Lord your God, am a jealous God, punishing the children for the sin of the parents to the third and fourth generation of those who hate me."*

Let's agree that the idea of a "generational curse" is frightening. Let's also agree that—without turning to God—messed up parenting leads to messed up kids which leads to messed up grandkids, and so on. Children do, in fact, repeat the sins of their mothers and fathers, but take heart: the sins of the parents are not an unstoppable curse. The cure is repentance. The cure is acknowledging, receiving, and responding to the love of God.

The clue to the power of love is found in the last four words of Deuteronomy 5:9, which clearly state that generational punishment

18. William Faulkner, *Requiem for a Nun* (Chatto & Windus, 1919), 85.

applies to *"those who hate me."* When the hate is removed, the curse is gone. The next verse confirms that God eagerly shows *"love to a thousand generations of those who love me and keep my commandments"* (Deuteronomy 5:10).

When it comes to overcoming any generational curse, our best choice as grandparents is to lean into that love. That's the only way to put our painful past behind us. Flee from hateful behavior such as hypocrisy, lying, idolatry, and being quick to judge. Let's think twice before we start pointing out how our children's parenting skills could be improved. That's often not helpful. Especially for your family, lead with love and celebrate victories. Claim your own generation as the first of a thousand generations who love God and keep His commandments.

WHAT ABOUT YOU?

Living in the light of God's love can and will open the door to healing emotional wounds from childhood, but there still may be some damage control you need to do.

Resolve to move forward as a better parent even now. At the right time, humbly acknowledge your mistakes to your adult children and ask for their forgiveness. (Maybe using as few words as possible.) Listen and allow your children to process the past and set the tone for the future. Respect boundaries. Be a positive role model. When asked, share wisdom with gentleness and humility.

DAY 46
GRANDPARENTING ONE-ON-ONE

"It is only with the heart that one can see rightly; what is essential is invisible to the eye."
—Antoine de Saint-Exupéry[19]

Rita and I have eight grandchildren. Randall and Rachel have two kids. Max and Meghan have three. Isaac and Kaitlin have three. Two girls and six boys, and they're all different. Contributing factors include birth order, parenting styles, temperament, genetics, and God-given character traits.

I love them all. I would trade my life for any of them. And, as I said, they're all different.

While researching for and writing this book of devotions, I have come to realize that I don't treat them enough like individuals. I try to. When the families come over or we go to their homes, I do attempt to connect, even for a moment, with each of them. Still, I know I could do better seeing each one of them for who they are, what makes them tick, and how I can specifically offer respectful, positive, and winsome encouragement.

As grandparents, it's much easier to have a "herd mentality." Especially on the rare and precious occasion when all eight grandkids and the rest of the family are together. Rita and I will typically manage the space and the food. The highlight for me is just standing on the sidelines watching the interactivity of all the generations.

As grandparents, taking it all in and appreciating the panorama can be wondrous. Cousins playing, laughing, competing. Moms, dads, aunts, and uncles recalling past mischief and catching up on the latest opportunities and challenges.

19. Antoine de Saint-Exupéry, *The Little Prince* (Harcourt, Brace, 1943), 87.

Come to think of it, family gatherings are not the time for a grandparent to seek out one-on-one time with a grandkid. The group dynamic is the priority.

Finding one-on-one time with a grandchild will require some intentionality. Have Mom or Dad pull out the family calendar. Inviting a grandchild to a concert, movie, theme park, or some costly event is certainly an option, but it doesn't have to break the bank. Whatever you do, just make sure you include time to physically and emotionally connect.

You can make it a win-win-win by embracing this idea as a chance for you to connect with your grandchild while also being of service to their mom and dad. It might be babysitting while the parents go on a date. It might be when Sophia's brother has a jam-packed Saturday, and you can rescue her from being dragged to all her brother's practices and appointments. It might simply be offering to pick up a middle schooler for an outing after school.

One-on-one time with a grandchild may be the only chance you have to see them with your heart, to uncover their otherwise invisible hopes, dreams, fears, and deepest desires. During your time together, they may even get to know you, which will serve you well in your final years on the planet. The relationship described in Ecclesiastes 4:9–10 can be a model for you and your grandchild: *"Two are better than one, because they have a good return for their labor: If either of them falls down, one can help the other up."*

Think of it this way. Like the shepherd in Jesus's parable of the lost sheep, we need to demonstrate that each child is precious to us. Whether they're hanging out with the rest of the flock or wandering on their own, let's make the effort to show them how special they are individually.

WHAT ABOUT YOU?

I hope you'll take this to heart. Begin a dialogue with Mom and Dad to help them see the benefit of that kind of one-on-one time. The goal is to build a relationship so that spending an hour, a day, a weekend, or longer with Grandma or Grandpa is something each kid wants to do.

THE FOURTH CHOICE

*You are as young as your faith, as old as your doubt; as young
as your self-confidence, as old as your fear; as young as your
hope, as old as your despair.*
—Dr. Frank Crane[20]

As a grandparent, there's a good chance you are anticipating or are
already engaged in some kind of retirement. For most seniors, the
single focus of retirement planning seems to be financial. You're
juggling Social Security, pensions, health care, debt management,
investment portfolios, housing, insurance, and so on.

Of course, financial planners have all kinds of recommendations
and warnings. You can probably find a good advisor from the recommendations of friends who have been through it. Look for someone
who returns your calls and welcomes you into their local office but
also has a diversity of investment options and national connections.
Maybe someone from church. That's the sum of my advice on your
finances.

At this season of life, more important than your wealth management is your mindset. Look around and you'll see three kinds of
retirees who get it wrong. As a result, they miss out on the joy and
opportunities of this season of life.

The first group says, "I'm old. Too old to be of any use." The
second group says, "I refuse to admit that I'm growing older," and
they embarrass themselves by going to tanning booths, wearing hip
clothing, and trying to act twenty years younger. The last group says,
"I've worked all my life, retirement is for me, me, me."

---

20. Dr. Frank Crane, "Society: Youth," *The Carlsbad* Argus, April 17, 1914,
https://www.newspapers.com/image/502812887/ .

For your sake—and the sake of your grandchildren—I recommend a fourth choice. That is to pray, "Lord, You've brought me this far. What's next?"

That might be all it takes to discover a surprising world of new joys and unexpected opportunities right in front of you.

In tomorrow's devotion, we'll brainstorm some possibilities. But the bigger point is this. Sure you've done much, but there's still so much more to do. The world, your neighbors, your friends, and your family—especially your grandkids—need you to stay in the race. By remaining open to God's plan, retirement can become a time of growth, contribution, and blessings.

WHAT ABOUT YOU?

If you were mentoring a young adult just starting out, you might hit them with the familiar words of Jeremiah 29:11, "'For I know the plans I have for you,' declares the Lord, 'plans to prosper you and not to harm you, plans to give you hope and a future.'" Grandma and Granddad, don't you think that this verse still applies to those in their fifties, sixties, seventies, eighties, and above? Maybe even more so!

DAY 48

GOD'S WORK

"Often when you think you're at the end of something, you're at the beginning of something else."
—Fred Rogers[21]

Congratulations on your retirement. Now what?

You've spent the last several decades storing up work and life experience, making connections with gifted people from all walks of life, learning that common sense is not very common, and honing your ability to see the big picture of what's really important.

As promised in the previous devotion, here's a list of ideas brainstormed just for you. However, don't limit yourself to what's printed here. Prayerfully free your mind to let these ideas trigger other ideas. Also, consider that many of these ideas you can do on your own, while others may involve collaborating with a business, nonprofit, or church.

Volunteer at a food bank or soup kitchen. Assist in disaster relief. Organize donation drives. Take weekly shifts at a local thrift store. Offer hospice support. Get certified in grief counseling. Start a beautification project in your own neighborhood or the city center. Plant trees and flowers. Plant vegetables in a community garden to give away or sell at the local farmer's market. Walk around the farmer's market and ask the vendors if they need a hand. Volunteer at an animal shelter. Join a home repair group. Attend a storytelling session at the local library. Take part in community theater. Record audiobooks for the visually impaired. Record songs for music therapy programs. Take cooking classes. Teach cooking classes. Teach

---

21. Fred Rogers, *The World According to Mister Rogers: Important Things to Remember* (Balance, 2024), 40.

digital literacy. Provide childcare for your grandchildren or the neighborhood kids. Start a childcare service for single moms. Assist homeschool families. Take or lead yoga, tai chi, Zumba, Pilates, or other fitness classes. Start a walking club. Join a service organization. Continue your career at your own pace by consulting, offering workshops, career coaching, blogging, or simply going part-time. Go back to school. Go to seminary. Assist refugees or immigrants. Go on a short-term mission trip. Move to an overseas mission field. Volunteer at a crisis pregnancy center. Volunteer at blood drives. Do prison ministry. Drive the elderly or infirm to medical appointments. Become a mentor. Advocate for veterans. Join a nonprofit board. Run for city council or school board. Write your memoir. Write a devotional. Create a podcast. Revisit an old hobby or start a new one. Turn your hobby into a business.

Your home church may have dozens of opportunities to volunteer: maintenance, lawn care, bookstore, office temps, set up and tear down, tech support, men's and women's ministry, small group coordinator, pulpit supply, Sunday school teacher, choir, keyboards, guitar, worship leader, greeter, prayer team, nursery volunteer, VBS volunteer, community outreach, hospital or homebound visitation, youth group volunteer.

It's okay to take your financial situation into consideration. Some of these activities are strictly voluntary, while others can supplement your cash flow nicely.

Finally, remember that staying active makes you a more interesting and inspiring grandparent. More on this ahead.

WHAT ABOUT YOU?

Continue and expand your brainstorm. Ask trusted friends to identify your gifts. Consider options that are the exact opposite of your previous career path. Ask "What if?" questions. Ask what you would do if money were no object. Ask WWJD? Fill a wall with ideas written on sticky notes. Try something easy and temporary to see where it might lead. Pray.

THROUGH THEIR EYES

The righteous will flourish like a palm tree, they will grow like
a cedar of Lebanon; planted in the house of the LORD, they will
flourish in the courts of our God. They will still bear fruit in old
age, they will stay fresh and green, proclaiming, "The LORD is
upright; he is my Rock."
—Psalm 92:12–15

When you look at your grandchildren, you simultaneously see the past, present, and future. You recall your own kids at that age. You agonize over the world in which they live, including school shootings, cultural decay, advancing technology, environmental deterioration, terrorism, and all sorts of dangers lurking around the corner. (Even as you also see a bright future with so much potential in their expressive eyes, curious questions, eager energy, and desire for your approval.)

When a young grandchild looks at you, they probably don't see the past, present, or future. They're too busy trying to figure out how to zip their jacket, open a juice box, fill a squirt gun, or replace the batteries in the drone remote control.

Mostly, when they look at you, they need to see a role model. They don't know it, but they need to see you thriving like the visual images in Psalm 92 above. That's growing, flourishing, and bearing fruit, even in old age. By staying *"fresh and green,"* you are proclaiming to those young people that *"the LORD is upright; he is my Rock."*

That is the Gramps and Grammy they want to hang out with and learn from. Displaying a zest for life—not being an old fuddy-duddy—is one of the main reasons they will trust you when you begin to share your faith with them and you dare to suggest spiritual answers for all those dangers mentioned above.

The previous devotion brainstormed specifics on how to stay active and interesting. This short entry moves beyond things to do, instead focusing on who you are. In other words, the personal qualities you need to embody to inspire and connect with those kids you love so much.

When young people are blessed with vibrant, interesting, and faithful grandparents, they will see you as a source of wisdom and guidance. They may be inspired to persevere and be fearless when it comes to creativity and push the boundaries. Inspired by your enthusiasm and inquisitiveness, their own curiosity will serve them well as they explore hobbies, extracurricular activities, and career options. Your unconditional love and acceptance will expand their own ability to love their neighbors. Seeing your home and companionship as a safe harbor, they'll gain a sense of security to explore the world, knowing they have a place that will always welcome them with a warm hug and a plate of homemade cookies.

In a nutshell, that's why, instead of saying, "I'm too old to be of any use," you should focus on flourishing. That doesn't mean pretending you're still under thirty. Instead, act your age because you've earned it. Old age is a wonderful, biblical time to bear fruit.

WHAT ABOUT YOU?

Are you finally embracing the idea that retirement is not all about you? Your children and grandchildren are watching. They need to know that the future is not all downhill, and the highlights of your day are not sitting in a recliner and talking only about the weather and your aches and pains. How you take full advantage of this fresh new season of life can serve as a guide for future generations and be a shining example of how to use your time, talents, and resources to advance the kingdom.

NOT-SO-FAMOUS QUOTES

A word fitly spoken is like apples of gold in a setting of silver.
—Proverbs 25:11 (ESV)

Sitting at my keyboard, pondering the role of grandparents, I am regularly overcome with emotion, appreciation, memories, dreams for the future, and an occasional regret.

These revelations sometimes make it into words that may be worth sharing on Instagram, jotting on a sticky note, or pausing to pray over. I've gathered a few of them here. Feel free to quote me!

When your kids have kids everything changes.

You never forget the way to Grandma's house.

Give your grandchildren so many memories they never run out of stories about how awesome you were.

A grandparent should be part teacher, part playmate, part secret keeper.

Grandparents can deliver a myriad of truths parents are afraid to speak.

There's no sweeter sound than a grandchild running through your front door calling your name.

Young people who know their heritage will honor their family.

Faded photographs come to life when shared with a grandchild.

Even in your quest to be the favorite grandparent, do your best not to pick a favorite grandchild.

Don't be surprised if being a grandparent finds you reevaluating many life decisions, including where you live, when you retire, and what people call you.

Standing in a pew next to your teenage grandchild singing "Amazing Grace" needs to be on your bucket list.

Kids need stuff only grandparents can give.

Grandparenting instincts are ninety-eight percent exactly right. Be wary of that two percent.

It's not a bad thing when your kids think of home as home.

Grandchildren may not sit at your feet and ask to hear your life story, but they yearn for that connection.

God made grandparents to be living history books.

The most valuable inheritance you can leave is your own embodiment of integrity, faith, and love.

A wise grandparent treats every grandchild differently. And the same.

You're only as old as your grandkids think you are.

It's not cool for a high school athlete to acknowledge a mom or dad in the bleachers. But grandparents get waves and smiles.

The best place ever to play is grandma's house and the best friend ever is grandpa.

Grandparents should always lead with love.

Few things are as satisfying as watching your children turn into parents right before your eyes.

What nickname will your grandkids give to your minivan?

When you know your grandchild, you know yourself.

Did you have any swings and misses as a mom or dad? Grandparenting just might be your chance for a do-over.

If you don't share God's love and faithfulness with your grandchildren, who will?

WHAT ABOUT YOU?

What words come to mind when you consider your own role as grandparent?

HOLD RULES LOOSELY

Remind the people to be subject to rulers and authorities,
to be obedient, to be ready to do whatever is good.
—Titus 3:1

Let me affirm that grandparents need to know and obey Mom and Dad's rules.

Little ones need to be in car seats. Photos of grandkids cannot be posted on social media without permission. You cannot take Molly to get her ears pierced or Hayden to get his first haircut. Meds need to be taken on time. If a grandkid has allergies, follow that protocol.

That being said, here are some family rules G-ma and G-pa can bend or even break. (Most are no big deal.)

Later bedtimes. Unlimited sweet treats. Extra screen time. Cookies on the couch. Veggies left on the dinner plate. Jumping on the bed. And so on. You can probably think of many others. Your list may even include quite a few things you didn't allow your own kids to do!

When this kind of anarchy breaks out at Grandma's house, there may be some fallout or questions. When they find out, Mom and Dad will most likely give you a look of exasperation, but they'll follow it up with words that let you and the grandkids off the hook: "Well, okay. But let's not make it a habit."

In the moment, the grandkids know they've been getting away with murder. Your one rule-following grandchild (probably an oldest child) may even say, "I don't think we're allowed to do that." That's when you can allay any fears and concerns with words of assurance: "I promise it's okay. The rules are a little different at Grandma's house."

A clarifying conversation may endorse the value and purpose of rules, and when rules can and should be broken. For instance, car seat rules keep kids safe. Roller coaster rules keep kids from falling out. No diving in the shallow end keeps kids from breaking their necks. Finishing homework before playtime allows you to enjoy playtime. Brushing twice a day helps prevent your teeth from falling out. Silencing cell phones makes movies bearable.

Like so many conversations, if it feels right in the moment, go ahead and remind your grandchildren that a certain historic figure was famous for breaking rules.

Jesus dined with tax collectors and sinners. He dared to talk to the Samaritan woman at the well. He touched lepers! Jesus healed the sick on the Sabbath. He was accused of blasphemy because He claimed to have the authority to forgive sins. (See Mark 2:15–17; John 4:1–29; Mark 1:40–45; Mark 3:1–6; and Mark 2:5–12.)

If the conversation and questions continue, you can then point out that the closer you are to Christ, the clearer you will be on which rules really matter and which ones you can break.

WHAT ABOUT YOU?

Of course, in some families, Grandma's rules are *stricter than Mom and Dad's.* That can work, too. In my case, visiting my grandparents, I lived in fear of leaving a smudge on Nana's white carpeting, leaving one of Grandpa's tools out of place, or spilling on the tablecloth at Easter. I would have been more eager to spend time at Nana and Grandpa's house with fewer rules.

TAKE A STAND

But as for me and my house, we will serve the LORD.
—Joshua 24:15 (NASB)

There's a good chance you've seen this verse on a wall hanging, fridge magnet, or welcome mat. Rita and I have it on a wall plaque in our living room. I confess that, years ago, when I first read this simple declarative sentence, I instantly appreciated the sentiment, but I had no idea of the context.

You may know the story. Moses had led the Israelites out of Egypt, carried the Ten Commandments down from Mt. Sinai, and wandered in the desert for forty years, but didn't quite make it into the promised land. He turned that privilege over to his God-appointed successor, Joshua. The military strategist led God's people across the Jordan River, tumbled the walls of Jericho, conquered a long list of kings, and won back the entire promised land of Canaan.

In the last chapter of the book of the Bible that bears his name, Joshua would call this next generation of Israelites to the plains of Shechem for a final farewell. He chose this spot because that's where God had promised the land to Abraham some four hundred years earlier. Speaking to the crowd, Joshua reminded them of the many historic events that had led up to that moment, all proving God's faithfulness. And then he offered this challenge:

So fear the LORD and serve him wholeheartedly. Put away forever the idols your ancestors worshiped when they lived beyond the Euphrates River and in Egypt. Serve the LORD alone. But if you refuse to serve the LORD, then choose today whom you will serve. Would you prefer the gods your ancestors served beyond the Euphrates? Or will it be the gods of the Amorites in whose land you now live? But as for me and my family, we will serve the Lord. (Joshua 24:14–15 NLT)

The book of Joshua ends hopefully. Three times, the crowd promises, *"We will serve the* Lord*"* (Joshua 24:21, 24; see also verse 18). Joshua died at the age of 110, a heroic warrior at peace with the assurance that the Israelites were firmly committed to the Lord.

But it wouldn't last. A mere two chapters into Judges, the next book in the Old Testament, we find Israel had not kept its promises and had returned to its idolatrous ways.

In a way, that's a reminder that, like the crowd that day—and all of us—we have a choice to make. There are many gods. And we need to choose every day whom we will serve.[22]

WHAT ABOUT YOU?

Can you—and the parents of your grandchildren—say, *"As for me and my house, we will serve the* Lord*"* (Joshua 24:15 ESV)? Moreover, will that declaration last?

---

22. Excerpted in part from Jay Payleitner, *The Next Verse* (Whitaker House, 2018), 20–22.

BE LIKE LOIS

Do your best to present yourself to God as one approved, a worker who does not need to be ashamed and who correctly handles the word of truth.
—2 Timothy 2:15

The following six verses from the opening of 2 Timothy may be the most revealing passage for grandparents in all of Scripture. Allow me to set the scene.

Paul is writing from a cold Roman prison, probably waiting to die. This second letter to his dear friend Timothy, who is like a son to him, contains the last recorded words we have from Paul. It has been years since these traveling companions have seen each other. The impact of these two men across much of the known world, including modern-day Turkey, Greece, and the Mediterranean, is unmistakable.

Paul is passing the torch. His tender words express gratitude to God and a promise of continued prayer. Paul calls on Timothy to not be timid but to *"fan into flame the gift of God"* (2 Timothy 1:6). Hidden in the opening paragraph of this landmark piece of writing is a real-life confirmation that the faith of a grandmother can help change the world.

To Timothy, my dear son: Grace, mercy and peace from God the Father and Christ Jesus our Lord. I thank God, whom I serve, as my ancestors did, with a clear conscience, as night and day I constantly remember you in my prayers. Recalling your tears, I long to see you, so that I may be filled with joy. I am reminded of your sincere faith, which first lived in your grandmother Lois and in your mother Eunice and, I am persuaded, now lives in

you also. For this reason I remind you to fan into flame the gift of
God, which is in you through the laying on of my hands. For the
Spirit God gave us does not make us timid, but gives us power,
love and self-discipline. (2 Timothy 1:2–7)

We really don't know much about Timothy's grandmother Lois
or his mother, Eunice. They are mentioned in the Bible only this
once, but I have the sense they weren't investing in young Timothy
for the fame anyway.

We do get one more glimpse of their dedication to sharing the
gospel with family members later in this letter. Paul writes, *"As for*
you, continue in what you have learned and have become convinced of,
because you know those from whom you learned it, and how from infancy
you have known the Holy Scriptures, which are able to make you wise for
salvation through faith in Christ Jesus" (2 Timothy 3:14–15).

Did you catch that? According to 2 Timothy 3:14–15, Lois and
Eunice had been sharing God's truth with the future missionary
since he was just an infant. Paul noticed and makes a direct connection between a grandmother's instructions and the gospel.

WHAT ABOUT YOU?

The Bible has a smattering of instructions for senior citizens.
They are instructed to pursue righteousness; to declare God's power
to the next generation; to be temperate, self-controlled, and worthy
of respect. Spoken and written instructions are valuable. However,
more effective than words, Lois serves as a real-life model we can
emulate today. That's a gift Lois gave to Timothy—and you.

THE GENERATION GAP

Every generation laughs at the old fashions,
but follows religiously the new.
—Henry David Thoreau[23]

The term "generation gap" was first used in 1967 by John Poppy, an editor for *Look* magazine, to describe the divide in politics, fashion, moral values, and the entire life perspective between the young and the old. Back then, "old" was anyone over thirty and "young" were the baby boomers, coming of age and disparaging their parents, who had grown up during the Great Depression and had sacrificed so much to win World War II.

However, the idea of conflicting and antagonistic differences between young adults and the older generation didn't begin in the 1960s. The popular notion of labeling generations and wrestling with their mutual hostility and distrust goes back to biblical times.

There's even a plan for ending any generation gap in 1 Timothy 5:1–2 (NLT): *"Never speak harshly to an older man, but appeal to him respectfully as you would your own father. Talk to younger men as you would to your own brothers. Treat older women as you would your mother, and treat younger women with all purity as you would your own sisters."*

Do you get the point? It's about respect, which goes both ways. Grandparents, you should expect the next generation to seek your experienced guidance. At the same time, you need to get rid of any know-it-all attitude. Come alongside your children and grandchildren as brothers and sisters, especially when it comes to appreciating their overall value as contributors and members of society.

---

23. Henry David Thoreau, *Walden* (Ticknor and Fields, 1854).

It may help to remember that all of us are made in the image of God. Every member of your family has dignity and worth. We all have the capacity for reason and creativity, along with an ethical responsibility to honor, admire, and even revere every other person.

Do residual signs of the generation gap show up in your family? In your church? Take a moment to reflect on your own youth and freely smirk at your certainty that you knew it all, only to realize much later that you still had much to learn. That idea may help you give a measure of grace and compassion to the upcoming generations.

As for the generation gap in your church among volunteers, worship styles, teaching series, leadership, discipleship, outreach, and Scripture interpretation? Your elders are likely well aware of the challenge. With your newfound appreciation for the importance of connecting the generations, see if you can be part of the solution.

WHAT ABOUT YOU?

What signs of dissent and distrust are you seeing between the generations? If you thought being a fun and awesome grandparent was the extent of your duties in this season of life, then surprise! Your next role could have you making critical connections between generations to strengthen and heal your church and beyond.

MOVING FORWARD WITH CONTENTMENT

Content makes poor men rich;
discontent makes rich men poor.
—Benjamin Franklin[24]

Early retirement, corporate downsizing, and other employment scenarios have left quite a few grandparents without work and *worried about their fixed income…or no income.*

An honest assessment of your savings, investments, expenses, and other cash flow factors may have left you with a spirit of fear and uncertainty. If that's the case, you'll want to be prudent with the resources you do have, seek new opportunities, stay connected with your circle of friends and colleagues, and trust in God's provision. Not to oversimplify or minimize your personal budget crisis, but, for Christians, a spirit of contentment is always within reach.

Philippians 4:11–12 reminds us of Paul's reassuring perspective: *"I have learned to be content whatever the circumstances. I know what it is to be in need, and I know what it is to have plenty. I have learned the secret of being content in any and every situation, whether well fed or hungry, whether living in plenty or in want."*

Part of that contentment can come as you find yourself with more time to spend with your grandchildren. Flying them to Europe or spending a week at Disney may not be in the budget. Still, the most worthwhile opportunities to invest in their lives require nothing more than time, creativity, and love. You can do that, right?

If that honest look at your finances reveals you can retire comfortably, you may find God has plans to make you uncomfortable.

---

24. Benjamin Franklin, *Poor Richard's Almanack* (U.S.C. Publishing Co., 1914), 18.

Perhaps with a second career in ministry. Does your church need help with men's or women's ministry? Or hospitality? Or homebound visitation? Or missions work? Your rewarding experience as a grandparent may have helped you realize that you should be active in children's ministry at your church. They can always use help!

Does the Salvation Army have a local chapter? Drop a note to "human resources" at your favorite national ministry and include your career history. Don't expect big bucks, but do expect great satisfaction.

Don't be concerned your second career or volunteering will take away from your time or enjoyment of your grandchildren. Just the opposite. You'll discover that taking time off from your new vocation is a bit easier than your old job. The good you're doing and the stories you'll have will make you an even bigger hero in the eyes of those young people who will be glad that you're making the world a better place.

WHAT ABOUT YOU?

You say you haven't heard God's call? Well, maybe He's using this chapter in this devotional to get your attention!

You say you don't think you have much to offer? Ask around, you'll find a ministry that needs your exact gifts.

You say you're tired and want to slow down? Understood, but there are still plenty of things to do that need to be done. Things that maybe only you can do.

VIEW FROM THE CHEAP SEATS

Anxiety weighs down the heart, but a kind word cheers it up.
—Proverbs 12:25

I know your grandchildren are the most talented, most athletic, smartest kids in the world. But for a moment, let's pretend they're not.

On your way to that gallery, gymnasium, field, theater, classroom, or auditorium, you have a certain set of expectations. You hope they will perform with excellence, shining brightly, so you can whisper to the stranger sitting next to you, "That's my granddaughter." Leaving your seatmate both impressed and envious.

However, in your heart, you know there's a chance your grandchild may not be a high performer. As a matter of fact, they might be terrible. (Or maybe they're still learning the basics, haven't blossomed yet, or need a bit more confidence.)

In the moment, there are four principles grandparents need to take into consideration.

First, there's a good chance the young performers are nervous. They're feeling the pressure from parents, coaches, directors, and themselves. They don't need more from you.

Second, before or after the event, the wrong words can set their head spinning or crush their little hearts. Steer clear of off-putting or dismissive remarks, or backhanded compliments such as "Don't be nervous," "Just do your best," "You were so much better this time. Maybe you'll do even better next time," or "Your friend Cameron is very good."

Third, assume Mom and Dad are already well aware of their child's talent and ability. (Or lack thereof.) Which means, you don't have to point out the misplays and missteps.

Fourth, the job of grandparents is to show up, applaud, and say, "I'm so glad you invited us." Or maybe, mention something that was legitimately outstanding: "I gotta tell you, I loved the second number."

If Mom and Dad want your sincere opinion at a later time, even then, be more than kind. The best course of action for that young-ster will soon be clear. Every kid has gifts, and you want them to keep trying new things until something really clicks. As their skills improve, you can be the first to recognize it and quietly let them know.

In 1 Timothy 4:12–15, we find Paul encouraging young Timothy to pursue and diligently practice his gifts of preaching and teaching, as well as modeling love, faith, and purity. In application, the princi-ples of encouragement and ongoing instruction apply to the pursuits of your own athlete or performer. Look up that passage together. Your budding Bible scholar will especially appreciate 1 Timothy 4:12: *"Don't let anyone look down on you because you are young."*

WHAT ABOUT YOU?

Attend all the performances, games, and exhibits you possibly can. Lean toward being a cheerleading observer. However, if you become a regular attender and have some legitimate expertise—along with a growing positive relationship with your grandchild—than some grandparents have the right and responsibility to step up as a valuable instructor or coach. The key might be to ask if they want your advice, then start simple.

THE MOST IMPORTANT THING

If I speak in the tongues of men or of angels, but do not have
love, I am only a resounding gong or a clanging cymbal. If I
have the gift of prophecy and can fathom all mysteries and all
knowledge, and if I have a faith that can move mountains, but
do not have love, I am nothing. If I give all I possess to the poor
and give over my body to hardship that I may boast, but do not
have love, I gain nothing.
—1 Corinthians 13:1–3

You want your grandchildren to do great things. You want to sit in the bleachers and watch them sink the buzzer beater, hit the walk-off homer, and stick the landing. You want them to graduate with honors and land a great job. That's your dream for them, right?

Even better, you want them to speak eloquently on spiritual matters, grasp the mysteries of God, possess faith that moves mountains, and be sacrificially generous on behalf of the less fortunate. Those are all character traits described in the first three verses of 1 Corinthians 13.

Reviewing that passage through until the final word, you can't miss the fact that—as wonderful as those character traits are—they don't have any value or meaning without love. Without love, each of us gains "nothing." We have nothing. We impact nothing. Our lives are nothing.

That's actually a bit frightening.

At our age, we can all look back and tick off a nice, long list of accomplishments. Why did we do those things? Was it for profit or personal glory, out of fear or curiosity, because our parents told us to, or because someone double-dog-dared us?

Remember, anything we do without love means nothing.

Makes you think, doesn't it? We absolutely want our grandchildren to set goals, take risks, work hard, solve problems, and make a difference. But, first and foremost, we want them to love.

By the way, what is love, anyway? Keep reading. We're digging deeper in the next few devotions.

WHAT ABOUT YOU?

Over your own life, I have a sense you've enjoyed some proud moments and checked off a lot of boxes. You may have received awards in elementary school for perfect attendance, sportsmanship, or being the classroom helper. You received a high school diploma, earned a degree, or a certification. You can recall your first paycheck, bonus, or promotion. At church, you volunteer and give sacrificially. Among friends, you're always there when they need a helping hand or a listening ear. With your family, you show up and want to be the best grandparent you can be. For your grandkids, well, you would do anything!

Was it—is it—all done with love?

DAY 58

LOVE IN ACTION

Love is patient, love is kind. It does not envy, it does not boast,
it is not proud. It does not dishonor others, it is not self-seeking,
it is not easily angered, it keeps no record of wrongs. Love does
not delight in evil but rejoices with the truth. It always protects,
always trusts, always hopes, always perseveres. Love never fails.
—1 Corinthians 13:4–8

You gotta love the "love chapter" of the Bible. These words are familiar to brides and grooms everywhere. Although it's popular at weddings, this description of what love looks like goes far beyond romantic love. After reading the passage a few times, you'll conclude it seems to emphasize that love is a decision followed by action.

Applying the love chapter to your role as a grandparent is not as easy as you may think. Sure, you love those kids, so you readily choose to be patient and kind, and not be easily angered. Of course, you are always hopeful and eager to protect. Over the years, you've also gotten good at persevering.

Some of the other love equations are more daunting. It feels right to boast about and be proud of our grandkids, but apparently boasting and pride are the opposite of love. For some of those rascals, keeping a record of wrongs would be beneficial because you can't "always trust" them.

Some pastors suggest this test. Replace the word "love" with your name. "Grandma is patient, Grandma is kind…Grandma keeps no record of wrongs…Grandma always protects, trusts, hopes, and perseveres." That sounds like a worthy and loving goal.

That strategy might even lead to a conversation with your grandchild. Especially after they say, "I love you, Grammy." Your response could be, "And I love you. Love is so great, but it's hard to describe, isn't it? Do you know what love is?"

Your grandkids—at any age—will look at you funny. But then they'll say, "Umm...I think so," or "Huh?" That's when you open your Bible to 1 Corinthians 13:4–8. Maybe even insert their name while asking if they are patient, kind, and all that.

Here's the bigger point. Grandparents have the rare and profoundly meaningful opportunity to be the embodiment of love, delivering an unconditional love that comes as close as humanly possible to the unconditional love of Jesus.

WHAT ABOUT YOU?

If you allow yourself, you should be making discoveries all the time in your regular study of the Bible. It takes a bit of creativity and courage, but you need to figure out a way to share some of those discoveries with your grandchildren. It might be sending a text or a link. Or it might require a bit of acting. When they come in the room, falling back in your chair and saying, "Wow, you won't believe what I just read." Then relate to them a verse or passage you came across this week or even one that has been important to you for decades.

DAY 59

LOVE DEFINED

God is love. Whoever lives in love lives in God,
and God in them.
—1 John 4:16

I think we need one more devotional on the topic of love. Mostly because you're overflowing with it, and you need to know the best way to deliver it to your family and inspire them to stir up their own supply.

We know that love is active and we know that certain activities express love. We also know that action without love is "nothing." Still, we have not yet landed on a definition.

At this point, we should acknowledge that the ancient Greeks identified four types of love, which C. S. Lewis described in his 1960 book, *The Four Loves*: storge, philia, eros, and agape. In layman's terms, that's (1) love for family akin to the affection of parental love; (2) brotherly love, or friendship; (3) romantic love leading to intimacy; and (4) unconditional love, which best describes God's nature.

The good news for most grandparents is that you've experienced all four kinds of love, saving the best for last: the unconditional love you have for your grandchildren. Not to say you don't love your own children unconditionally, but sometimes the busyness, parental concerns, and battling the culture wars got in the way.

Unconditional (agape) love is what Christ is talking about in John 15:13, *"Greater love has no one than this: to lay down one's life for one's friends."* He's not talking about family, friends, or romance. He's talking about dying to yourself, living for others, and loving your neighbor more than you love yourself. In other words, the kind of love Jesus showed on the cross.

May I go so far as to suggest that you would die for the well-being of your grandchildren? I'm fairly sure I would, if given the choice. (Maybe because they've each got eighty years of life ahead, and my best years are behind me! But that's beside the point.)

The real point is this: God is love. God's love is unconditional. Showing unconditional love to your grandchildren will help them—at the right time—to understand and accept God's love as demonstrated on the cross. There are quite a few people on this planet who continually hold God at arm's length because they don't think they are worthy of God's love. When your grandchildren experience and feel your unconditional and even sacrificial love, you have taken away that potential barrier. That's love worth sharing.

WHAT ABOUT YOU?

Have you experienced God's unconditional love? It's pretty hard to give love if you have not accepted love. Maybe go back and re-read all of 1 Corinthians 13.

THINGS YOU KNOW

The fear of the LORD is the beginning of knowledge, but fools despise wisdom and instruction.
—Proverbs 1:7

Young people may be light-years ahead of us when it comes to gaming and some technology, but take heart—there are quite a few things you know that they don't. Here's just a partial list.

You know how to write in cursive.

You know that naps are desirable.

You know how to change a tire.

You can find and identify the Big Dipper, Orion's Belt, and the North Star.

You know that God created everything in the universe.

You know how to make a paper airplane that actually flies.

You know how to make a campfire. (And how to make the perfect s'more.)

You know the value of compound interest.

You know to tighten the lid before shaking a bottle of salad dressing.

You know all the words to "Piano Man," "Sweet Caroline," and "Amazing Grace."

You know life goes on when the internet goes out.

You know God knows everything. (Even more than Google or Wikipedia.)

You know how to whistle with two fingers.

You know to save your work before closing a document on your laptop.

You know how to tell time on a clock with hands.

You know God's timing is perfect.

You know that if it moves and it shouldn't, use duct tape; if it doesn't move and it should, use WD-40.

You know the seven dwarves, the seven deadly sins, and the seven castaways.

You know to treat others the way you want to be treated.

You know the first step in completing a jigsaw puzzle is to find the edge pieces.

You know to check the expiration date before drinking from a carton of milk.

You know how to read an actual map to get to your destination.

You know that Jesus is the Way, the Truth, and the Life. (See John 14:6.)

The list could go on and on. Frankly, there are some things your grandchildren will never know. The important stuff—the stuff that needs to stick—will be learned during teachable moments. For example, when you happen to be outside with them on a clear night, is when you point out a few constellations. Don't stop there. Go ahead and explain how God *"determines the number of the stars and calls them each by name"* (Psalm 147:4).

When the internet goes out, tell the kids you can't always count on Google, but you can count on God. Pull out an old road map and see if they can find the best route to their hometown, then ask if they know the way to heaven.

You get the idea. You know things that can help them navigate through life, and you know even more important spiritual insights that lead them into the next life.

WHAT ABOUT YOU?

Do you see God at work in the world around you? That's what you need to share with your grandchildren! The best spiritual lessons aren't when you sit them down for doctrinal formation. Young people will learn to know and love God when they see His love, care, and guidance working in real life.

DAY 61
IDENTIFY A KEEPER OF THE CALENDAR

There is a time for everything,
and a season for every activity under the heavens.
—Ecclesiastes 3:1

Rita just left for an evening Kiwanis's meeting and I will soon be heading to Reese's softball game. I know Reese has a softball game because the handwritten note on our kitchen calendar says. "Reese SB 6:30."

It's a great system. Rita puts all her meetings and all the grandchildren's activities on a calendar next to the fridge. I know what's going on because it's right there, out in the open, serving as a confirmation and reminder. Yes, it's also on my iCalendar phone app, but seeing it handwritten in plain sight still feels right. (Plus, every once in a while, an event doesn't make it onto the phone app.)

When it comes to our local grandchildren, we don't make every event. I get tons of joy watching them participate in baseball, softball, wrestling, football, tae kwon do, and even the ubiquitous and monotonous game of soccer. But I recommend you *don't* attend all of them. Traveling teams, especially, may have dozens of games in a season. If you show up to all of them, parents and kids start taking you for granted. They need to appreciate your efforts, especially attending out-of-town games. Missing a game should never produce any grandparental guilt.

On the other hand, most onetime events are can't-miss, and that includes end-of-year band concerts, all-star games, plays, science fairs, award ceremonies, and so on. In general, if your grandchild's name is going to be announced from a podium or over a loudspeaker, be there to cheer and applaud.

All that to say, I need to give my own round of applause to Grama Rita for making it easy for me to know what's going on and when. Her motivation may have been because she wanted to stop my pestering her with, "Hey, what's going on tonight/tomorrow/this weekend?"

Nonetheless, the system works. Despite what the next generations think, grandparents often have full schedules, and staying in communication keeps us in sync and on time.

Even though we're not talking about money, Proverbs 21:5 seems to apply here: *"The plans of the diligent lead to profit as surely as haste leads to poverty."*

So, whichever way works for you sync your schedules, with your spouse and your kids. Add smartphone apps that give travel directions, weather alerts, ticket information, parking reservations, and local dining options. Suddenly, the entire experience can have less haste and expense than when our own kids were in extracurricular activities.

WHAT ABOUT YOU?

You may be a novice when it comes to lacrosse, wrestling, the cello, madrigal singers, lyrical dance, one-act plays, robotics, poetry slams, anime, Model UN, and other activities in which your grandchild might be participating. Go anyway. You'll probably enjoy it. They'll know you care. Ask that young artist or athlete a few legitimate questions, and you might give them the honor and joy of teaching you something. Some events are so significant that out-of-town grandparents may want to get on a plane just to be a part of them.

DAY 62

GOOD GRIEF

The LORD is close to the brokenhearted and saves those who are
crushed in spirit.
—Psalm 34:18

Let's talk about grief. As an optimist, I can usually face loss or heart-ache with a long-term vision that includes hope, recovery, and ulti-mately gratitude for the person, place, or thing that has been lost. But let's face it, by the time you're a grandparent, you're entering a season of life when losses have a tendency to accumulate. We know lots of people, and stuff happens.

Grief comes from obvious and unexpected places. You've almost certainly had friends and family members pass away. Whether that's suddenly or after a long illness, grief is to be expected. It's permis-sible. The closer you were to that individual, the more intense and long-lasting the grieving process will be. Circumstances surround-ing some deaths become almost unspeakable or horrifying. The acci-dental death of a young person. Suicide. Murder. Terrorism or mass shooting. A fatal overdose. The death of a newborn or SIDS.

Guilt, regret, agony over unfulfilled dreams, anger, confusion, helplessness, and other extreme emotions are natural responses. It's unfortunate, but a common response is separating yourself from others who are hurting, which happens at the exact time you should be coming together to console each other and share your grief. A Swedish proverb explains, "Grief shared is halved, joy shared is doubled."

Be warned: grief also comes from inevitable life events such as leaving a job, selling your family home, friends moving away, a child moving cross country, putting down a pet, a beloved pastor retiring, or even a favorite restaurant closing. Just this week, we had to cut down a favorite climbing tree in our side yard; the loss and flood of memories brought me to tears.

Here's the point for grandparents. With the next loss you face, be sad. Don't hide or dismiss your grief. In a mindful and age-appropriate way, share your feelings with your grandchildren. Let grief take its course. Effectively and efficiently going through the classic stages of grief—denial, anger, bargaining, depression, acceptance—will help you today and model for your family the best way to accept and respond to their own inevitable seasons of grief.

We know that heaven will bring complete relief from grief. Revelation 21:4 promises, *"He will wipe every tear from their eyes. There will be no more death or mourning or crying or pain, for the old order of things has passed away."*

The Bible also has lots of insight to share with your grandchildren today, before they face the grief of a friend moving away or getting cut from the basketball team. One verse young people appreciate for its high-flying imagery and message of resilience is Isaiah 40:31: *"Those who hope in the LORD will renew their strength. They will soar on wings like eagles; they will run and not grow weary, they will walk and not be faint."*

WHAT ABOUT YOU?

Today, take to heart the three verses quoted in this devotion on behalf of your grandchildren and yourself. Don't wait until you're hurting. You already know that sorrow and suffering are part of the human experience. Embracing and memorizing Psalm 34:18, Revelation 21:4, and Isaiah 40:31 will serve you well in your own times of grief and as a grandparent connected to the Creator of the universe.

DAY 63

OFFERING ADVICE

Is not wisdom found among the aged?
Does not long life bring understanding?
—Job 12:12

Many of our sons and daughters are in their thirties or forties, and you remember what that means: change, and lots of it. Their careers, homes, cars, kids, marriages, and health are all in transition. As a result, they are constantly experiencing good news and bad news, beginnings and endings, challenges and opportunities.

When they share that news—if they share it—our first instinct is to offer advice. After all, much of what they're enduring, you already experienced.

Without a doubt, you have all kinds of wisdom to share on parenting, finances, home buying, car buying, marriage, lawnmowing, wallpapering, grilling salmon, flossing, the best brand of peanut butter, and how to hang a new roll of toilet paper.

Job 12:12 even confirms that our life experience has blessed us with abundant wisdom and understanding. However, before gracing them with your aged insight, reflect on this amusing passage from Matthew 7:6: *"Do not throw your pearls before pigs, lest they trample them underfoot and turn to attack you"*(ESV).

This is not to suggest that your adult children are swine and eager to attack. But some of your pearls of wisdom may be antiquated, out of touch, completely ineffective, or even dangerous. It's disturbing to consider, but our generation's advice on car seats, home remedies, vaccinations, and the best way to put an infant to bed could literally put lives at risk.

How can you best be of service to your children when it comes to offering parenting wisdom? If you've sensed a recurring theme in this devotional, you won't be surprised to hear it's all about listening, empathy, respect, patience, and staying available to those young parents.

Start by reminding yourself that (1) you made parenting mistakes, (2) they will make parenting mistakes, and (3) that—unless it's life-threatening—you need to honor their final say when it comes to how they raise their kids.

Rather than giving specific advice, try storytelling, even saying "I'm not sure about now, but this is how we did it back in the day." That leads to safe and open discussion that initiates valuable give-and-take. In some cases, you might humbly suggest you have some ideas and ask if they want to hear your perspective. Please don't be surprised or upset if they say no.

WHAT ABOUT YOU?

Often, giving advice to your adult children is all about timing—but we even get that wrong. Responding to a need, we instantly recommend action steps, when actually it might be better to quietly come alongside and match their emotions. Just be with them. Romans 12:15 suggests, *"Rejoice with those who rejoice, and weep with those who weep"* (NASB1995). Celebrate victories and share their brokenness. Empathy creates partnership.

BREAKING BREAD

"To speak gratitude is courteous and pleasant,
to enact gratitude is generous and noble,
but to live gratitude is to touch Heaven."
—Johannes A. Gaertner[25]

Flip through your Bible, and you might be surprised at how often profound moments unfold around the simple act of sharing a meal. Consider Passover, Jesus's first miracle at the wedding in Cana, the Last Supper, Abraham preparing a meal for three visiting angels, the feast celebrating the return of the Prodigal Son, the miracle of the loaves and fishes, and Jesus dining with tax collectors and sinners.

In the book of Acts, communal meals are tied to three foundational practices: teaching, fellowship, and prayer. Acts 2:42 says, *"They devoted themselves to the apostles' teaching and to fellowship, to the breaking of bread and to prayer."* When you look at that verse in context, you'll see it is nestled between two monumental events for the early church. The previous verse confirms that three thousand new members of the church were baptized. The verse that follows describes how *"everyone was filled with awe at the many wonders and signs performed by the apostles"* (Acts 2:43).

Who knew that something as simple as sharing a meal could play a part in such world-changing events?

That brings me to a recommendation for grandparents. Before you downsize, make sure you still have room—or at least a plan—for gathering your clan. A few times a year (more or less) you'll want to

25. Johannes A. Gaertner, *Worldly Virtues: A Catalogue of Reflections* (Phanes Press, 2002), 19.

gather all or most of your family for fellowship. For some reason, that works best around a big table. Especially around holidays.

In my home, for more than twenty Thanksgivings, I fashioned an eight-foot-square table out of two laminated sheets of plywood to seat nearly two dozen guests. Around that table—over the centerpiece and a lavish feast—the entire tribe shared eye contact, laughter, love, and so much more.

A welcoming dining table becomes a sacred place, a place of blessing. As necessary, it can be a place of brokenness, forgiveness, and welcoming strangers. Before partaking of any meal, join hands and give thanks to God for His provision. Applaud the meal preparers. Share stories of the day, the season, or the year. When a milk glass tumbles, don't make it a big deal.

If you gather with open hearts, the act of breaking bread can even have healing power. Even in the best of families, hard feelings and division can creep into relationships, for reasons both serious and silly. Yet it's remarkable how a long silence between siblings or old friends can come to an end when one of them simply says, "Can you pass the potatoes?"

WHAT ABOUT YOU?

In too many families, holidays have become a time of regret, divisiveness, resentment, and unspoken tension. At best, conversation is polite but distant, each word chosen carefully to avoid stirring old wounds. Is there something you can do to restore love, joy, respect, and promise? Let's explore some options in the next devotion.

HANG TIGHTLY TO TRADITIONS

Civilization is impossible without traditions, and progress impossible without the destruction of those traditions. The difficulty, and it is an immense difficulty, is to find a proper equilibrium between stability and variability.
—Gustave Le Bon[26]

One activity worth engaging in with your grandkids is to list family traditions. This is an especially amusing exercise for your teenage grandchildren, who may be beginning to push away from family activities, but still desperately cherish traditions. Pay attention and you'll notice that teenagers are the first to notice (and be upset) when a tradition changes, whether it's swapping out the centerpiece, topping the Christmas tree with a new star, changing the rules on the Easter egg hunt, or skipping the first-day-of-school photo.

For the Payleitner family, traditions that have gone on uninterrupted season after season include backyard campfires, Thanksgiving football, multiple deliveries of Peeps from kids to my wife at Easter, Christmas stockings hung by the chimney with care, a family movie outing between Christmas and New Year's, and texting Grama when you get to your destination safely. All those we still do.

We also still count on Rita's ever-changing decor for holidays, which includes Valentine's Day, St. Patrick's Day, Memorial Day, and Independence Day. We don't decorate for Halloween, but we certainly carve pumpkins, and Rita has custom-designed and sewn dozens of costumes from Superman to Ringmaster to a Rockford Peaches uniform. A few grandkids come by each December to bake cookies. And there's always a full pew at the Christmas Eve service.

---

26. Gustave Le Bon, *The Crowd: A Study of the Popular Mind* (Dover Publications, 2002), 46.

On the other hand, there are quite a few cherished traditions we've let slide for one reason or another. For decades, most of our kids and grandkids gathered for fireworks on July 4 at the local golf course. This past July, it was just Rita and I at a different location. The rest of the family was scattered at gatherings with friends and in-laws watching different fireworks displays. Original Christmas skits featuring my five children and six cousins had a solid fourteen-year run. As a teenager, Rae Anne was no longer enthusiastic about delivering May baskets to neighbors. Several times every summer, our four boys (actually adult males) found themselves playing stickball in our driveway. That stopped five or six years ago. The annual multigenerational softball game ended when my dad passed. Sibling photos with Santa ended when our eldest, Alec, turned twenty-one.

As you can imagine, when our nest emptied, it made perfect sense that several traditions instantly vanished. That realization was a legitimate, even heartbreaking, loss. But it also led to this conclusion worth sharing: *Hold tightly to traditions, but recognize when it's time to let a tradition go.*

WHAT ABOUT YOU?

As you compile your own list of traditions that have come and gone, take note of any you can revise for your grandchildren! All it takes is to reflect on when your own children were the age your grandkids are now. Can you picture your own kids—years ago—caroling, apple picking, volunteering, building a gingerbread house, delivering Christmas cookies, attending opening day of your favorite professional team, or visiting the same pumpkin patch, fishing hole, tree farm, sledding hill, or beach, year after year? Put it on the calendar. And expect a flood of memories and gratitude from your grown children.

DAY 66

PLAYGROUND WISDOM

He makes my feet like the feet of a deer;
he causes me to stand on the heights.
—Psalm 18:33

Have you noticed? Playgrounds are cooler and more attractive than ever and often include a variety of innovative features such as climbing walls, ropes courses, curvier slides, and interactive play panels. In our hometown, Rita and I recently attended the dedication of a playground with inclusive attractions, including a wheelchair-accessible swing!

For better or worse, the more dangerous elements you may remember from your own youth have been eliminated. That includes rusty monkey bars that invite kids to climb ever higher...and eventually lose their grip. Kid-propelled merry-go-rounds that demonstrate centrifugal force and leave kids flying across yards of gravel. And, of course, the killer seesaw that leaves one kid instantly dropping eight feet to the ground when the other kid decides to get off. How did we survive?

Let's applaud school and park districts that create environments for all kids that are both challenging and safe. Let's also be aware that the existence of colorful, inviting, and ubiquitous playgrounds can be a bit frustrating for parents. Boys and girls are drawn to them. Moms and dads just don't have time.

Today's parents have a lot on their plates, but you can't blame a five-year-old for asking to go to the park. Even if a mom or dad gives in their child's request, their myriad responsibilities are never far from their mind. In some ways, today's parents never feel free to fully engage with their children.

You've witnessed the scene at one of the many parks in your area. A youngster energetically climbs, hangs, swings, leaps, and monkeys all over a giant colorful structure. Meanwhile, Mom or Dad is sitting or standing forty feet away, engrossed in their phone, texting, talking, or checking emails.

That might seem like a parenting fail, but let's pause before passing judgment. As a bystander, we don't know the full story. That digital communication could be urgent, and we should commend that parent for even bringing their kid to the park.

Instead of judging, let this scene serve as a reminder of our own God-given purpose as grandparents. Our season of life probably allows us a little more time, a few less distractions, a bit more flexibility, and a surplus of hard-earned wisdom on how to prioritize and see the bigger picture.

While our physical stamina and flexibility may have waned, we can make up for it by offering undivided attention to something as basic as a visit to the playground.

WHAT ABOUT YOU?

The personal application from this devotion may simply be "take your grandkids to the park." More than that, I hope the picture painted above helps you remember and realize the different seasons of life, how swiftly the time passes, and the challenges and opportunities facing each generation.

And—oh, yeah—you may be over fifty, but you can still climb, swing, and slide, too!

GET A ROCKING CHAIR

Be still, and know that I am God.
—Psalm 46:10

Maybe you already have one. You may have acquired your first rocking chair when you brought home that first bundle of joy a million years ago. If it was well-made and well-kept, you might still have it. It could be on your front porch or back patio, or still in your family room. Maybe you recently moved it into the newly redecorated guest room that was once a teenager's pigsty of a bedroom.

That rocking chair may have been a place for nursing a newborn, thinking deep thoughts, waiting with a shotgun for your daughter to come home from the prom, recovering from an illness or surgery, or rehearsing for old age.

The very act of rocking—especially while soothing an infant— leads to the comforting realization that there is more to life than the here and now. Much has been said and written about seizing the day and striking while the iron is hot. However, a rocking chair serves as a physical reminder of the value of slowing down.

It's a cliché, but there are reasons older folks like to sit on the front porch and rock. The fresh air. Just enough "exercise" to keep the blood moving. The elevated vantage point to see what's going on in the world. Greeting visitors as they stroll past. And, as described in Psalm 46:10, being still, praying, and listening to God. Knowing Him.

With that thought, let's all look forward to being the kind of senior citizen who rocks, prays, loves, remembers back, and looks ahead with a sense of gratitude, and humbly shares wisdom with all we meet.

This idea is so fundamental to the role of a grandparent that I recommend doubling or tripling down on your rockers. Get a second identical rocking chair for your spouse, friend, or teenage grandchild so they can join you in quiet conversation and wisdom sharing. Also, get a smaller version for that youngster who emulates everything you do.

I am 100 percent sure we could use a little more stillness these days. Not just to know God, but to exalt Him. That is confirmed in the second part of Psalm 46:10. After reading *"Be still and know that I am God,"* we are promised: *"I will be exalted among the nations, I will be exalted in the earth."*

You may not have realized it until now, but sitting quietly in your rocking chair offers you one of the best chances to know God and exalt Him among all the nations on earth.

WHAT ABOUT YOU?

Stillness is almost impossible these days. Distractions are constant. We wear busyness as a badge of honor and confuse activity with progress. The loudest voice gets our attention. The squeaky wheel gets the grease. The most obnoxious social media gets shared. Buzzing smartphones beckon us constantly. Is stillness possible? Go ahead and try it. Twenty seconds of silence, even now. If that works, try being still for twenty minutes, or twenty days.

FIFTEEN SHAREABLE FUN FACTS

We know that "We all possess knowledge."
But knowledge puffs up while love builds up.
—1 Corinthians 8:1

Some truths hold more value than others. As a matter of fact, possessing knowledge can make a person feel pretty important, when what they really need is a bit more empathy and compassion. Still, at a certain age, most kids become fascinated with trivia and superlatives. You can use that curiosity to engage them in spiritual truths.

Try sneaking these facts into everyday conversation. Or sit down with your middle school-aged grandchildren and ask them if they'd like to know fifteen true and fun facts.

1. The sun is a star. It's just one of billions of stars in the galaxy. It's just closer, that's all!

2. Ice floats. However, 90 percent of an ice cube or an iceberg is still underwater.

3. A giraffe's tongue is black. Their prehensile tongues, which can be up to eighteen inches long, are dark to protect them from sunburn. Prehensile means their tongues can grasp on to leaves and twigs.

4. Jesus and John the Baptist were second cousins. Their mothers—Mary and Elizabeth—were first cousins.

5. Henry Ford introduced the Model T in 1908. The first traffic light in the U.S. was built in Cleveland, Ohio, in 1914.

6. The South Pole is in Antarctica. There is no land at the North Pole—just ice.

7. Jesus's ministry only lasted approximately three and a half years. The exact amount of time to change the world.

8. A polar bear's fur is not white. Its fur is actually transparent and hollow, but it looks white because it reflects visible light.

9. Hummingbirds are the only known birds that can also fly backward. That's how they flit in and out from flowers or feeders.

10. The speed of light is fast enough to circle the earth seven times in one second. That's 186,000 miles per second.

11. Butterflies taste with their feet. Sensors on their feet help them find food by landing on plants.

12. Jesus's tomb was triple-protected by a large stone, a Roman guard, and a Roman seal.

13. Bamboo stalks can grow more than three feet in one day.

14. Whales are mammals, not fish. Despite living in the ocean, whales breathe air, give birth to live young, and nurse their babies with milk.

15. The human body has approximately 60,000 miles of blood vessels. That's long enough to circle the earth about two and a half times!

Did you learn something? Do you now have some fascinating facts to share with your most curious grandchild? Will you?

WHAT ABOUT YOU?

I trust you noticed that three facts about Jesus of Nazareth were part of this list of fun facts. That idea points to this critical realization for Christian grandparents: talking about Jesus should be a natural part of your interaction with your grandchildren. He is at the center of all that matters. But don't make it a lecture. The joy comes when you're laughing and learning about all kinds of things, and the conversation naturally transitions to spiritual truths.

OUR GENERATIONAL GOD

You, LORD, reign forever;
your throne endures from generation to generation.
—Lamentations 5:19

You may be quite familiar with the comforting concept that God knows and cares about each of us as individuals. Scripture makes that abundantly clear.

> *Before I formed you in the womb I knew you, before you were born I set you apart.* (Jeremiah 1:5)

> *Can a mother forget the baby at her breast and have no compassion on the child she has borne? Though she may forget, I will not forget you! See, I have engraved you on the palms of my hands.* (Isaiah 49:15–16)

> *Suppose one of you has a hundred sheep and loses one of them. Doesn't he leave the ninety-nine in the open country and go after the lost sheep until he finds it? And when he finds it, he joyfully puts it on his shoulders and goes home.* (Luke 15:4–6)

These verses affirm that before you were born, as an individual child of God, and even when you feel lost, He knows you and is looking out for your best interests. But an abundance of other passages confirm that God is also caretaker, comforter, and King of multiple generations. Including your kids, grandkids, and beyond.

> *Your faithfulness continues through all generations; you established the earth, and it endures.* (Psalm 119:90)

> *Know therefore that the LORD your God is God; he is the faithful*
> *God, keeping his covenant of love to a thousand generations of*
> *those who love him and keep his commandments.*
> (Deuteronomy 7:9)

> *Your kingdom is an everlasting kingdom, and your dominion*
> *endures through all generations.*   (Psalm 145:13)

Finally, one of the most remarkable confrontations between God and man serves as a memorable reminder of God's connection to the generations. Early in the book of Exodus, at the burning bush, God instructs Moses to take off his sandals and then identifies Himself by identifying Moses's ancestry.

> *"Do not come any closer," God said. "Take off your sandals, for*
> *the place where you are standing is holy ground." Then he said,*
> *"I am the God of your father, the God of Abraham, the God of*
> *Isaac and the God of Jacob." At this, Moses hid his face, because*
> *he was afraid to look at God.*   (Exodus 3:5–6)

You see, dear grandfather and grandmother, you don't live for yourself. God's Word and sometimes the voice of God Himself will speak to future generations and point back to your faithfulness.

WHAT ABOUT YOU?

When your name is written in the Book of Life (see Revelation 3:5), you become connected to Abraham, Isaac, Jacob, and Moses. Bible scholars even suggest that you become part of the *"great cloud of witnesses"* (Hebrews 12:1) described in chapters 11 and 12 of Hebrews. What a privilege and delight it will be to watch future generations throw off sin and *"run with perseverance the race marked out"* just for them.

DAY 70

STUFF IS OVERRATED

Do not store up for yourselves treasures on earth, where moths and vermin destroy, and where thieves break in and steal. But store up for yourselves treasures in heaven.
—Matthew 6:19–20

Remember the time you elbowed through an army of shoppers to get your hands on that hot new toy for your grandchild, only to realize by Christmas morning that they already had one—and were already tired of it? How about the countless hours spent deciphering tech reviews to ensure you were getting the "coolest" gadget, only to have your grandkid roll their eyes when they opened it because they knew it was obsolete technology.

It's easy to get caught up in the whirlwind of wanting to give our grandkids the latest and greatest. We've all been there: frantically searching online for the perfect gift, battling holiday crowds, and even succumbing to last-minute impulse buys that seemed like a good idea at the time. Our motivation is to be the best grandparent ever.

But let's be honest. How many times have those carefully chosen gifts ended up collecting dust, forgotten in a corner, or overshadowed by the next big thing? The truth is, our grandchildren might not remember the specific toys or gadgets we gave them, but they will remember the love, grace, and kindness we showed them.

Think back to your own childhood. The memories that stand out are probably not about the things you had but the moments you shared. The bedtime stories, the lessons learned, the laughter, and the feeling of being cherished. These are the treasures that last a lifetime—and beyond.

While I don't typically suggest Christians follow cultural trends, a recent survey leading up to the Christmas holidays by GetYourGuide deserves our attention. The global online marketplace found that a staggering 92 percent of Americans would rather receive experiences to share with loved one over physical gifts.[27]

Jesus taught us to store up treasures in heaven, emphasizing the importance of the intangible, eternal things over the temporary, material ones. When we focus on embodying love, grace, and kindness, we create lasting memories and impart values that will stay with our grandchildren long after the fading appeal of any gizmo or toy.

WHAT ABOUT YOU?

Today, instead of stressing about the absolutely perfect gift, focus on creating near perfect experiences. Spend time with your grandkids, listen to their stories, share your own, and show them unconditional love. Simple and sincere acts of love and grace are the true treasures you can give. Absolutely buy your grandkids gifts for holidays and birthdays. But don't stress about it, because the best gift you can give doesn't come from a store; it comes from your heart.

27. GetYourGuide Press Team, "New GetYourGuide Survey Finds a Staggering 92% of Americans Would Rather Receive Experiences Over Physical Gifts This Holiday Season, Reinforcing the Increasing Desire to Create Lasting Memories with Loved Ones," October 18, 2023, https://www.getyourguide.press/blog/new-getyourguide-survey-finds-a-staggering-92-of-americans-would-rather-receive-experiences-over-physical-gifts-this-holiday-season-reinforcing-the-increasing-desire-to-create-lasting-memories-with-loved-ones.

DAY 71

JOY IN THE JOURNEY

*Being confident of this, that he who began a good work in you
will carry it on to completion until the day of Christ Jesus.*
—Philippians 1:6

This verse seems especially appropriate for grandparents. It reinforces one of my primary messages to seniors that shows up elsewhere in this book. You've done so much, but there's still so much more to do. (You can quote me on that.)

You gotta love Philippians 1:6. It's a promise that any good work you've begun will be completed. That's empowering. That's invigorating. And that's only part of the story.

The first dozen times I read this verse, I missed the point. (Can you relate?) I thought Paul was cheering me on for "my" good work. I thought that I would *"carry it on to completion,"* thereby earning all the glory and applause. But that's not it at all. Read it again.

It's God who began the work. It's God who will complete it. Yes, He wants our partnership. He wants us to dream big dreams, get our hands dirty, and enjoy the sweet smell of success. However, make no mistake: nothing happens unless God orchestrates the entire turn of events.

Paul wrote this letter to the church at Philippi from a jail cell. He begins by thanking the members of the active church there, including overseers and deacons. He acknowledges their dedication to sharing the gospel and promises to keep them in his prayers. The rest of the book—just a few pages—is all about joy. Joy in serving, believing, giving, even joy in suffering.

The book of Philippians overflows with memorable passages:

For to me, to live is Christ and to die is gain.
(Philippians 1:21)

Do nothing out of selfish ambition or vain conceit. Rather, in humility value others above yourselves, not looking to your own interests but each of you to the interests of the others.   (2:3–4)

Brothers and sisters, I do not consider myself yet to have taken hold of it. But one thing I do: Forgetting what is behind and straining toward what is ahead, I press on toward the goal to win the prize for which God has called me heavenward in Christ Jesus.   (3:13–14)

Rejoice in the Lord always. I will say it again: Rejoice!   (4:4)

Do not be anxious about anything, but in every situation, by prayer and petition, with thanksgiving, present your requests to God. And the peace of God, which transcends all understanding, will guard your hearts and your minds in Christ Jesus.
(verses 6–7)

I can do all this through him who gives me strength.   (verse 13)

Written from a jail cell, the book of Philippians is an instruction manual for finding joy. But it doesn't begin with work, ambition, seeking your own personal interests, or our own strength. Joy begins with humbling ourselves before God.

WHAT ABOUT YOU?

When you're with your family, is it all about you? Grandparents who want to blaze their own trails may need a dose humility and a recommitment to their dependence on God. Then we can point any and all members of our family to our Creator as the true Source of joy.

ALEC'S SONG

[Speak] *to one another with psalms, hymns, and songs from the
Spirit. Sing and make music from your heart to the Lord.*
—Ephesians 5:19

I unexpectedly ran across a photo this morning that caught me off
guard. I gasped when I saw it. The memories came rushing back.

It's my mom and dad seated facing each other, holding hands,
and singing. Behind them is my oldest son, Alec, at the piano. The
occasion is a party celebrating Mimi's eightieth birthday, held at the
home of my sister Sue and her husband, Dwight.

As a gift, Alec had written a song called "They Just Don't Make
Mimis like This Anymore." I would describe it as a rollicking bar-
room polka, and the twenty of us all quickly picked up on the chorus,
singing along.

> I beg you to look
> Search the highest of highs
> And search the lowest of lows
> And you will only find
> CHORUS:
> That they don't make Mimis like this anymore
> They just don't make Mimis like this
> She'd give all she had for a moment of our happiness
> They just don't make Mimis like this
> Search over the river
> Search through the woods
> And you'll never find
> A Mimi that could
> Make the best chocolate brownies,

Let us put up her tree,
Take care of our Papa,
And put up with me!
She's queen of this motley crew
That's all gonna sing along
Cause what better way to show our love
Than to finish, finish this song?

For the record, Alec is a gifted songwriter and typically writes lyrics with multiple layers of meaning. But this song was exactly right for the occasion, and the applause was long and sincere for both the songwriter and his grandparents. Then someone pulled out an old songbook, and Alec played several memorable tunes on request. My folks began to sing *to each other*. Something I don't think I had ever seen before.

Here's the point. Over the years, Mom and Dad (aka Papa and Mimi) went to a ton of games, concerts, plays, award ceremonies, and other events. They even went to a downtown bar where Alec's rock band played pretty loudly. Because they showed up for the grandkids, Alec and his siblings and cousins all showed up for them.

As I type this, I'm sitting here weeping. Missing my parents. And I am so grateful to Alec and my entire family.

The lesson? Keep showing up. Be there for your family and friends. It all comes back around. A few years later, Alec added a couple of bonus verses on behalf of my folks' sixtieth wedding anniversary.

There's one fellow here
Knows better than anyone else
How she keeps us together
And never thinks of herself.
For sixty years now,
A marriage designed from above.
Together with Papa
She shows how to love.

WHAT ABOUT YOU?

Are you showing up? Are you worthy of a creative composition—music, words, dance, sculpture, recipe, quilt, jewelry, carving, photo collage, poetry—dedicated and presented to you by one of your grandchildren? It's not something you can request. It has to come from their heart overflowing with love and appreciation.

KIDS' CHURCH VOLUNTEER

You are the salt of the earth.
—Matthew 5:13

I wasn't sure if any kids would actually show up. That Sunday morning, windchills of twenty and thirty below zero swirled outside, and I was the volunteer scheduled to lead the large group teaching of elementary kids in the cheery basement of my home church.

I had been given the assignment to teach on Matthew 5:13–16 from the Sermon on the Mount. Like you, I was familiar with the passage. Still, I reread it a few times, meditating on how to relate the core message to a bunch of six-, seven-, and eight-year-olds. When the large group teaching time began, I introduced myself, made lots of eye contact, and with enthusiasm and warmth said, "Let's talk about salt! Tell me some things about salt!" Hands shot up across the room.

I knew the answers I was shooting for. (You probably do, as well.) Even if I didn't hear it from my young crowd, I would make sure that we landed on the facts that salt brings out flavor and acts as a preservative. I expected to take those answers and apply them to how Christians should live in the world.

In kid-friendly terms, I was prepared to teach:

"Like putting salt on a pretzel, following Jesus should make life more tasty and delicious."

"Mary and Joseph didn't have a refrigerator! Salt keeps food from going rotten."

What did the kids say that Sunday morning, and how did I respond?

"Salt is white."

"Excellent!"

"It's small."

"Yep! A little bit of salt goes a long way."

"It makes things taste better."

"Yes! We're going to talk about that!"

Then came a couple answers I wasn't ready for.

"Salt is bad for you."

"Umm? Yeah, I guess. Eating too much salt is not a good thing."

"It melts ice on the sidewalk."

"Wow!"

That bonus use of salt was a teaching point I had not considered. But as a student of improv and a speaker who loves audience interaction, I jumped on that idea!

"Yes, salt melts ice! There was salt on the sidewalk when you arrived at church today. Each of you can be like salt that melts the cold heart of anyone who feels a little grouchy. Even someone who gets grouchy like me! Your smile. A little hug. Saying something nice. Being kind. Jesus wants you to do things that melt cold hearts! Let's say a neighbor, your mom, dad, grandparent, or anyone is having a bad day. You can be salt! You can melt their grumbling or sadness!"

For me and for them, it was an unforgettable interaction. We went on to talk about how each of them can also be the "light of the world." We even sang "This little light of mine...."

WHAT ABOUT YOU?

I hope you can imagine yourself engaging a group of young people at your church as I did on that frosty winter morning. Grandparents may be the ideal group of volunteers to hold babies, entertain preschoolers, teach school-age kids, or challenge teenagers. So here are my three instructions from this devotion: Be salt. Be light. If it's in you, volunteer in the children's or youth programs at your church.

Then be prepared to learn something yourself!

A WINNING LESSON

The simple believe anything,
but the prudent give thought to their steps.
—Proverbs 14:15

As an occasionally silly and engaging grandfather, I'm going to take the next two pages to provide an example of how my mind works. Feel free to borrow this idea. It's part play, part competition, part con job—and it's a pretty solid life lesson.

Let's say you're walking with your first- or second-grade grandson or granddaughter to the playground. (This happens to me when their older brother or sister is participating in an organized sporting event on an adjacent field. At halftime or during the fourth inning, I'll grab the hand of the younger sibling and we'll head toward the colorful jungle gym/slide/climbing wall.)

When the two of you are about fifty yards away, say, "I'll race you to the slide." They'll like that idea, and there's a good chance they'll take off running. But when you don't run at all, they'll stop. Especially if you shout, "Slow down! Slow down!"

Your goal is not to outrun them; it's to outwit them. Continue to walk slowly and steadily while telling them, "I'm going to win, but you go ahead." Inevitably, their strategy will be to stay a few steps ahead of you. You can run for a bit, but don't pass them. About ten steps away from that tree or playground equipment, they will think they've won the race. That's when you distract them with words like, "Wow, I'm getting tired," or "It's a nice day for a race, isn't it?" Then, timed perfectly, sprint those last few steps, beating them by just half a second.

They might say "Not fair," or they may squeal with laughter. Either way, you have earned the right to say, "I told you I'd win."

What's the lesson? Well, you're not trying to break their trust or make them angry. But you are giving them several lessons in the way the world works. (1) The race isn't over until it's over. (2) It's not always the fastest or the strongest that get ahead. (3) In a competition, have a strategy for success. (4) Grandpa is a shrewd dude, and you may want to be on his side when the going gets tough.

A few weeks later, initiate that same race again. You might fool them a second time, but I can guarantee you won't win a third time. That's probably the bigger point. When they claim victory in future races, tip your hat and give them credit.

Finally, if they're old enough, you can even use your cunning ways to remind them that they need to stay on their toes. You don't want them to live in fear or distrust of people who should be trustworthy. But they do need to learn that the culture and the world can be a bit tricky, so they need to stay sharp, stand by their convictions, and make good choices.

WHAT ABOUT YOU?

In Matthew 10:16, Jesus tells His disciples, *"I am sending you out like sheep among wolves. Therefore be as shrewd as snakes and as innocent as doves."* Such advice doesn't surprise you. You've seen it all. But if you can initiate a conversation with your curious grandchild about the dangers of the world, you might save them a lot of heartache.

BE SELFISH

He gives strength to the weary and
increases the power of the weak.
—Isaiah 40:29

Let's get selfish for a moment. Yes, your grandkids benefit from your love, wisdom, encouragement, and all the other amazing stuff you do for them and with them. Yes, moms and dads appreciate when you take the little rug rats, snarky grade schoolers, and eye-rolling teens off their hands for a while. But—if you give it a chance—you can come out way ahead in this relationship, getting more personal benefit out of time spent with your grandchildren than you ever imagined.

Consider your health and wellness. Young people can be exhausting. That's good news! Keeping up with their active lifestyle gets your blood flowing, muscles moving, and brain working overtime. Play hide-and-seek, toss a Frisbee, or catch some lightning bugs, and your immune system, muscle tone, and heart health all get a boost.

Your emotional and psychological well-being also gets a kick start with every engagement. As they learn, play, pretend, imagine, and try new things, you will find yourself learning, playing, pretending, imagining, and trying new things. Initiate activities that generate laughter, and your cognitive function increases while your risk of depression and stress levels decreases.

Finally, you begin to see the world through a new lens. You're not dwelling on past mistakes or thinking that the best of life is behind you. Instead, you're seeing how your grandchildren's curiosity and daily discoveries are drawing them (and you) toward the future.

Of course, goofing with your grandchildren is not really being selfish. It's about living in the light of God's love. Sharing joy. Finding rewards in relationships. When you allow yourself to bask in God's faithfulness, your entire family benefits.

With that concept fresh in your mind and heart, go ahead and memorize Psalm 100:5: *"For the* LORD *is good; his steadfast love endures forever, and his faithfulness to all generations"* (ESV).

WHAT ABOUT YOU?

What are you doing for your physical and mental health? How many diets have you begun unsuccessfully? Do you own any gym equipment gathering dust? Are you popping pills or listening to self-help gurus to reduce anxiety? What if you simply spent more time engaging with your grandkids instead?

A REASON FOR EMPATHY

Finally, all of you, be like-minded, be sympathetic, love one another, be compassionate and humble.
—1 Peter 3:8

You have a grandchild. Or maybe a bunch. I'm delighted for you and hope they bring you great joy and are part of a legacy that impacts the world. I have eight grandkids, and I believe they will be a force for good in the world. Bringing solutions, not problems.

Judah, Jack, Emerson, Gideon, Reese, Nolan, Finn, and Nixon didn't exist fourteen years ago. Now I can't imagine a world without them. I enjoy thinking about them, hanging out with them, and imagining their future—even after I'm long gone. I also enjoy talking about them and showing off photos.

Yet, after a few painful conversations, I've learned to hold my tongue and—in quite a few interactions with other seniors—maybe not even mention my grandchildren at all.

As much joy as your grandkids may bring you, that's how much quiet agony is being experienced by an increasing number of people over sixty who are desperately longing for grandchildren and—in increasing numbers—don't anticipate ever having any.

Statistics from Pew Research Center reveal that a little more than half of adults fifty and older had at least one grandchild in 2021, down from nearly 60 percent in 2014. What's more, the trend of young adults remaining childless is increasing rapidly. From 2018 to 2023, the number of U.S. adults younger than fifty without children who say they are unlikely to ever have kids rose from 37 percent to 48 percent.[28]

---

28. 2023 Pew Research Center's American Trends Panel, Wave 133, August 2023, https://www.pewresearch.org/wp-content/uploads/sites/20/2024/07/PST_2024.7.26_adults-without-children_W133_topline.pdf.

For those of us with a vibrant crew of grandchildren with whom we interact regularly, let's choose empathy. Not pity. Not sympathy. But let's be compassionate and tenderhearted toward siblings and friends who may never experience grandparenting. Let's have a healthy awareness that our sharing about what's going on in our family may sound like bragging. Our celebration may lead to a kind of mourning. In many cases, they're glad for us, but quietly brokenhearted for their own circumstances.

In a similar category are grandparents who live far away from their grandchildren, as well as grandparents who have been cut off—for any number of reasons—from their grandchildren. They are experiencing a difficult, although hopefully temporary, kind of loss.

In most of these cases, there's not much we can do about it. As a compassionate Christian adult, your instinct may be to come alongside and help them talk through their pain or sorrow. However, in this case, that may not be the best approach. Any talk from you on the topic of grandchildren may open emotional wounds and add to their heartache.

Finally, being aware of this epidemic of heartache should lead you to overflow with appreciation for each and every one of your own grandchildren.

WHAT ABOUT YOU?

Despite the trend described above—or maybe because of it—you may have friends and family members without grandkids who graciously and genuinely ask about what's going on with your brood. Hearing about the achievements and seeing photos of your extended family might bring them joy, not sadness. In that spirit, you might even invite those loving souls to picnics, parties, or holiday gatherings where they can experience the unique satisfaction of hanging out with young people who represent the future. Creating opportunities for friendship, laughter, and connection to span across the generations is always a meaningful choice.

DAY 77

A FOLDER FOR SHOW

He will turn the hearts of the parents to their children, and the
hearts of the children to their parents; or else I will come and
strike the land with total destruction.
—Malachi 4:6

Most grandparents have half a billion unorganized photos on their phones. If you're like me that includes photos of glorious sunsets, grocery lists, model numbers off broken appliances, crafting ideas, prescription bottles, hailstones the size of quarters that landed on my front lawn, and, yes, a few pics of real-live people.

My favorites are the ones of my grandkids. Some I took myself. Many were sent from my thoughtful daughters-in-law, Rachel, Megan, and Kaitlin. And, of course, my favorite activity related to those photos is showing them off. For too long, each time I pulled out my smartphone, I would scroll through row after row of images, never quite finding the photo I was looking for.

That's when I came up with the best idea in this book. Grandparents, on your smartphone, create an album called "FOR SHOW." Keep fewer than a dozen photos in it. Select clear, current pics that show your family members with their best face forward. Literally. Because everyone knows how to swipe through photos, you can open that folder anytime and hand your phone to a new friend, colleague, or airplane seatmate. Then simply state, "Here's my family. Go ahead and swipe through. It's just ten photos." The exchange is so user-friendly, it doesn't even feel like bragging.

What's more, that "FOR SHOW" folder gives you instant access to every member of your family in no time at all.

When you carry, look at, or share photos of your family, wonderful things happen. Your heart softens. You are reminded of those loved ones as individuals. You are more likely to imagine what they are doing in that moment and to pray for them.

Your grandchildren may live nearby, and you see them regularly. Or they may live several states away. Regardless, their faces in your phone will help you hold them close.

Take a few minutes this week to gather and organize the ten photos that represent your kids and grandkids. (And maybe your dog.) If we ever meet—in an airport, bistro, church, or speaking event—go ahead and pull out your phone and click on your "FOR SHOW" folder. I'll show you mine, if you show me yours.

WHAT ABOUT YOU?

The idea of sharing photos of your grandkids—or even bragging about them—needs to come with a warning. As described in the previous chapter, many folks our age look like they might be grandparents, but they aren't. You might meet someone and make that assumption, which leads to a friendly question about their grandchildren. More often than we realize, that simple question can stir some heartache. It might be about grandchildren they never see, grandchildren lost to tragedy, or about a yearning for their adult kids to finally make babies.

So, proceed with care when it comes to forcing photos of your grandchildren on others. But feel free to view them often yourself—always adding prayers of gratitude, protection, and God's guiding hand in their lives.

YOUR MEMOIRS

Our theology must become biography.
—Tim Hansel[29]

In publishing, some of the best-selling books for grandparents are not books at all. They're journals with prompting questions. After a page or two of introduction, these journals are mostly blank pages meant for grandparents to fill in with lessons learned, personal memories, and wisdom for future generations. I recommend you do this.

Pursued with honesty and perseverance, the practice of journaling can allow you to leave a living history that would minister to many future generations. For sure, you'll want to mention any awards, accolades, and achievements for which you have been recognized, and reflect on the discipline and work it took to be so honored. In these keepsake journals, there's typically also room to document important dates, locations, key relationships, and milestones. But, the most compelling pages of your memoir would be your personal stories—the turning points in your life.

There's something that feels substantial and permanent about completing one of these legacy memoirs. How you choose to present it to future generations is up to you. Once completed, you may be tempted to secure it in some safe deposit box to be opened and read after your passing. I think a better idea is to share it with loved ones soon after you finish, polish, and proofread each section.

Your self-discoveries and stories can impact your grandchildren in real time. When they read how one specific high school teacher inspired you, they'll begin to see their own teachers in a new light.

29. Tim Hansel, *Holy Sweat: The Remarkable Things Ordinary People Can Do When They Let God Use Them!* (Word Publishing, 1987), 29.

When they read about how you hit bottom, leading you to finally cry out for salvation, they'll realize that God will meet them in their brokenness. How you overcame temptations, failed romances, broken dreams, and even frustration with God will be top of mind when they go through the same challenges. Journal about your past life victories with humility and gratitude, and you can celebrate them all over again—this time with family members who weren't even born then.

Don't forget to include favorite inspirational quotes and Scripture verses that have had special meaning in your life. If you approach this journal as an instructional tool for your children or grandchildren, you can't go wrong with Proverbs 3:5–6: "*Trust in the* LORD *with all your heart and lean not on your own understanding, in all your ways submit to him, and he will make your paths straight.*" Matthew 6:33 might also be included: "*Seek first his kingdom and his righteousness, and all these things will be given to you as well.*"

As an author, I can confirm that when you sit down at a keyboard and pray for inspiration that will impact others, God is pleased. Your words will have meaning and purpose.

WHAT ABOUT YOU?

Want to test this idea? Write a two-page letter to your eldest grandchild. Share a memory from when you were their age. Don't make it preachy. Make it a friend writing to a friend. Type it. Print it. Mail it. Email it. Whatever feels right. (If you write in cursive, there's a 50/50 chance your grandchild won't be able to read it!)

No matter what, you'll get some positive feedback that may inspire you to write your family's favorite book.

IT'S A GOOD TRADE

Therefore we do not lose heart. Though outwardly we are wasting away, yet inwardly we are being renewed day by day.
—2 Corinthians 4:16

When your feet hit the floor in the morning, do you immediately begin cursing the inevitable aches and pains of advancing age? Maybe you don't curse, but are you distraught about your blurred vision, tummy troubles, crackle-and-pop knees, and back strain from sneezing too aggressively the day before?

I hope you realize that our waning strength is all part of God's design. How so, you say? Well, our mortality and the breakdown of our bodies may be a consequence of the fall. Remember God's reprimand to Adam?

By the sweat of your brow you will eat your food until you return to the ground, since from it you were taken; for dust you are and to dust you will return. (Genesis 3:19)

Plus, as our bodies weaken, we get a dose of humility and a helpful reminder that we are dependent on God. That's all part of His plan to prepare us for eternity and inspire us to model for others what it means to have an eternal home waiting for us.

But our citizenship is in heaven. And we eagerly await a Savior from there, the Lord Jesus Christ, who, by the power that enables him to bring everything under his control, will transform our lowly bodies so that they will be like his glorious body.
(Philippians 3:20–21)

Praying for strength to carry out our earthly mission is also on our to-do list.

> *Do not cast me away when I am old; do not forsake me when my strength is gone.*   (Psalm 71:9)

Above all, we can and should have confidence that we are making an amazing deal. We may be wasting away, but we're simultaneously being renewed in soul and spirit. As described in Isaiah 64:6, we are trading old, filthy rags for new ones. Even our best human efforts are unclean compared to the renewal God has promised.

> *Therefore, if anyone is in Christ, the new creation has come: The old has gone, the new is here!*   (2 Corinthians 5:17)

WHAT ABOUT YOU?

Are you ready for the judgment? Have you traded your old self for a new life in Christ? You need to be ready now. Our life on earth is a finger snap when compared to eternity. In fact, your grandchildren also need to be prepared. When they're facing an earthly challenge or temptation, feel free to explain to them that the glory that awaits them in heaven more than makes up for any hassles or even any persecution we may endure on earth. *"For our light and momentary troubles are achieving for us an eternal glory that far outweighs them all"* (2 Corinthians 4:17).

SELF-FULFILLING PROPHECIES

Do not be deceived: God cannot be mocked.
A man reaps what he sows.
—Galatians 6:7

My dad was an elementary school principal for more than thirty years. Outside his office, he posted this well-known poem by Dorothy Law Nolte. You've probably seen it, although it may not be as well-received today as it once was.

Children Learn What They Live
If a child lives with criticism, he learns to condemn.
If a child lives with hostility, he learns to fight.
If a child lives with ridicule, he learns to be shy.
If a child lives with shame, he learns to feel guilty.
If a child lives with tolerance, he learns to be patient.
If a child lives with encouragement, he learns confidence.
If a child lives with praise, he learns to appreciate.
If a child lives with fairness, he learns justice.
If a child lives with security, he learns to have faith.
If a child lives with approval, he learns to like himself.
If a child lives with acceptance, and friendship,
he learns to find love in the world.[30]

Nolte wrote and published the original version in 1954, about the time my dad began his career as an educator. As a boy, I was drawn to the truths in her words whenever I stopped by his school office. Later on, I connected this poem to the idea that many human character traits stem from "self-fulfilling prophecy."

---

30. Dorothy Law Nolte, "Children Learn What They Live," https://www.childrenlearnwhattheylive.com/.

That term likely originated from the study of modern sociology with roots in the mid-twentieth century. But I believe it's a biblical principle that parents and grandparents can use for good. The concept that we reap what we sow affirms the idea that ridiculing a child can lead to shyness, encouraging a child leads to confidence, and so on. Proverbs 11:25 tells us, *"A generous person will prosper; whoever refreshes other will be refreshed."*

Real-life examples of self-fulfilling prophecies are easy to imagine. If a young student gets the idea that math is hard, they will likely put in less effort, and their grades will show it. A parent who doles out fair punishments will raise children who have a sense of justice. Grandparents who build a home filled with love and acceptance will have visitors who want to be there.

As it turns out, words, actions, and attitudes have consequences.

WHAT ABOUT YOU?

Can you identify any generational curse or blessing being passed down to your grandchildren and even future generations? There are all kinds of things you can do to break the curse or nourish the blessing. It begins with an honest reflection on your parenting style back in the day. In any case, don't wallow in any guilt or take credit for any blessings. But do ask God where you should go from here.

ABOUT YOUR PARENTS

Anyone who does not provide for their relatives,
and especially for their own household, has denied the faith and
is worse than an unbeliever.
—1 Timothy 5:8

If you're a youngish grandparent, there's a good chance your own parents are still around, which translates to an entire additional set of challenges, expectations, stresses, and opportunities. Perhaps on a daily basis.

As great-grandparents—now in their seventies, eighties, or nineties—your mother and father are passing on the generational baton. Decisions and obligations now falling on your shoulders have far-reaching implications.

You and your siblings likely will be making difficult decisions about your parents. That includes their living arrangements, the disposition of their old house, and their long-term accommodations. Along with that comes health care, medications, and even the task of transporting your parents and in-laws to doctors' appointments. Additionally, there are numerous financial decisions to consider, such as establishing a power of attorney and estate planning.

It's not just time-consuming, it's exhausting. And it's potentially fraught with conflict between siblings and other family members. Consider yourself warned.

If you find yourself in this position, also consider yourself blessed. You've been given the opportunity to give back to your parents, set some precedents, and model appreciation, devotion, and loyalty. Approaching this season of life with patience, generosity, and humor will be a great gift to your entire family.

You may find yourself making regular visits to the house in which you grew up, a place to which your parents downsized, or some kind of retirement village. When possible, drag along one or two of your own grandchildren. Great-grandparents need to see evidence of their unfolding legacy.

Wondrous things can happen when a six-year-old interacts with a great-grandparent. Not to reinforce stereotypes, but there's a moment in the arc of those two life spans when a youngster may be learning new things and an octogenarian may be forgetting a few things. All of which means, they can be equal companions on the road of life. Those two family members—separated by three generations—may find common ground talking about the deliciousness of a dish of sherbet, tracking the intricacy of a spiderweb, or laughing at geese honking overhead.

Parents, teenagers, and most family members don't have the time or patience for such silly distractions. But with a little preparation and patience, you can orchestrate those satisfying moments between your grandchildren and your own parents.[31]

WHAT ABOUT YOU?

Especially when school-aged grandkids tag along back to the old homestead or retirement center, try to ask your mom or dad open-ended questions to help uncover a few unspoken memories. Too often, those times together feel forced and include way too much talk about the weather, today's news headlines, or their latest physical ailments. Young people don't want to hear any of that. Keep the conversation going until the elder member of the family tells a story or two that even you have never heard before. Don't delay. Those memories fade when you least expect it.

---

31. See Payleitner, *Hooray for Grandparents!* 147–150.

ONE-MINUTE PIANO LESSONS

Mighty things from small beginnings grow.
—John Dryden[32]

Due to the bus schedule, our local school district decided that elementary school begins at 9:00 a.m., which means that hundreds of kids in town need to find a safe place to hang out for an hour and a half before the start of their official school day. With a mix of duty, delight, optimism, and purposefulness, Grama and I said we would be glad to entertain our third-grader, Reese, every morning before driving her to school.

Every morning, like clockwork, Rita engages our beautiful, silly, athletic, and oh-so-smart granddaughter at the kitchen table for about forty-five minutes. Then I wander down the stairs and begin what has become a fascinating and delightful ritual. After being slobbered on by our golden retriever, I grab coffee, shuffle to my office just off the kitchen, and speak my first utterance of the day: "Five-letter word." Reese skips into my office, and we begin conquering "Wordle," courtesy of the *New York Times*. If you don't know, the goal of the online game is to guess a five-letter word within six tries. We haven't lost yet, almost always nailing it in four tries or less.

Then Reese says, "Piano." This is shorthand for a phrase that I coined at the beginning of the semester: "One-minute piano lesson." While I am extraordinarily gifted with words, I have very little expertise at the piano. (I do appreciate music and played guitar a bit in my youth.) At my request, Rita dug through our ancient basement archives and found a beginning piano book complete with cartoonish illustrations, step-by-step lessons using variations of "Old

---

32. John Dryden, *Annus Mirabilis: The Year of Wonders, 1666* (Henry Herringman, 1667), stanza 155.

MacDonald" and "Twinkle, Twinkle," and an abundance of stickers and gold stars awarded to our eldest son, Alec, decades ago by a real piano teacher who knew what she was doing.

Turning pages in that book, Reese and I are learning together basic principles of piano, including music theory, finger placement, scales, and patience. And it's working! The daily, very brief, laughter-filled lesson is never painful for either of us. Just the opposite. In the other room, Rita—who took years of legit piano lessons back in the day—rolls her eyes as she endures our merrymaking.

I don't know how long this will continue or what Reese's musical future might be. We'll continue to do our best despite my lack of piano experience and an ancient instrument that has three, maybe four, broken keys.

Here's the point: small beginnings, faithfully executed, can lead to great victories. Bible readers will recognize this concept reflected in the growth cycle of a mustard seed, the dividends of investing first-fruits, and the potency of five smooth stones when taking on a giant.

The principle of starting small can also be found in the parable of the talents (see Matthew 25:14–30) when the master tells his faithful servant, "*You have been faithful with a few things; I will put you in charge of many things. Come and share your master's happiness!*" (verse 23).

WHAT ABOUT YOU?

Your time with your grandchildren may be plentiful or limited. Even if you only have a few minutes here and there, see each engagement as an opportunity to bless, learn, laugh, share your wisdom, and sometimes even reveal your own vulnerability. Everyone wins.

NO WHINING

Do everything without complaining or arguing.
—Philippians 2:14 (NLT)

Decades ago, as a joke, we installed a lovely wooden sign above a door in our kitchen that featured this two-word expectation: "No Whining." For the most part, our five children were never prone to extensive whining, but when Rita and I ran across the carved plaque at a local gift shop, it seemed appropriate in a lighthearted way.

As we approached our empty nest season, that sign became completely irrelevant. Alec, Randall, Max, Isaac, and Rae Anne were all too busy imagining and creating their futures. On the occasion when one of them came home and sat at our kitchen table, Rita and I were more than eager to hear about anything that was going on in their lives. A little whining about a boss, teacher, coach, or coworker was actually welcome. As you know, parents cherish updates from their maturing children regarding their career path, hobbies, wellness, and social engagements. We want to hear the good and the not-so-good.

When our adult kids happened to engage in some justifiable whining, Rita and I were excellent sounding boards. Not that we had all the answers, but we could offer a bit of empathy and—when asked—we had wisdom from experience that was sometimes worth hearing.

Which leads us to today and begs the question, "Which member of the Payleitner family is most likely to need the two-word reminder on that wooden plaque?" The answer is me.

When a publisher turns down a timely book proposal, I might grouse a bit. When clients request a fourth revision on a script or an ad campaign, a grumble or two may be forthcoming. When technology does what technology does, that certainly deserves a burst of wailing and yowling. Can you relate?

Honestly, whining of any kind is rarely helpful. Nor is it appropriate for an authentic Christian, especially when grandkids might be within earshot. As role models for younger generations, we need to demonstrate how God is constantly working in us and how we strive to live clean and innocent lives without complaint, shining bright even among nonbelievers. Here's how Paul put it:

> *Work hard to show the results of your salvation, obeying God with deep reverence and fear. For God is working in you, giving you the desire and the power to do what pleases him. Do everything without complaining and arguing, so that no one can criticize you. Live clean, innocent lives as children of God, shining like bright lights in a world full of crooked and perverse people.*
> (Philippians 2:12–15 NLT)

We're going to leave that pithy plaque up in the kitchen. When necessary, we'll even point it out to a grandchild. And I promise to keep this passage from Paul close to my own heart and share it with anyone who needs a friendly reminder of the downside of whining, including me.

WHAT ABOUT YOU?

What are your favorite adages or mottos? Even if they're not direct quotes from the Bible, they likely have roots in Scripture. "Actions speak louder than words." "Give credit where credit is due." "What goes around comes around." "Slow and steady wins the race." "No whining." (See James 2:18; Romans 13:7; Proverbs 26:27; Proverbs 21:5; and Philippians 2:12–15.)

THE VALUE OF PAUSING

A voice from heaven said, "This is my Son, whom I love; with
him I am well pleased."
—Matthew 3:17

Rita and I were both raised in a traditional church environment. Following the practice of our upbringing, our five children were all baptized as infants. The ceremonies were meaningful and joyous.

Over the years, we never missed a Sunday, developed a warm and gracious relationship with the pastoral staff, invested time and resources, and built many lifelong friendships through our church family. Still, we came to the conclusion that our young family needed more Bible teaching and less ritual. We needed to count more on convictions and less on traditions.

Our parents were not delighted to see us leave their denomination, and we understood where they were coming from. But once we had moved to the big nondenominational church on the edge of town, we knew it was the right decision. We soaked up the in-depth Bible teaching and dug into small-group studies. We also witnessed adult baptisms for the first time.

For many readers, that may seem almost routine. You may see adults being baptized several times per year. But you should know that for people who grew up in other traditions, it can actually be a bit startling.

After getting plugged into youth group, our oldest son, Alec, came to the conviction that he wanted to get baptized to demonstrate publicly that he had put his faith and trust in Jesus. Rita and I encouraged him, but we didn't know how that would sit with our more traditional parents. We considered celebrating Alec's baptism quietly, avoiding any uproar that might cause with grandma and grandpa.

Here's the point of this little story. (And I hope the lesson rings true for all grandparents.) Surprising Rita and me, Alec invited his grandparents to the ceremony! When he told his grandfather that he was going to get full-immersion baptized, my dad's initial reaction was a picture of grace and thoughtfulness. Simply stated, he paused.

Undoubtedly, it took my father by surprise. But after a brief moment, he finally said, "Well, if it was good enough for Jesus, it's good enough for my grandson."

I will be eternally grateful to my dad for that thoughtful, compassionate, and generous response.[33]

WHAT ABOUT YOU?

When one of your children or grandchildren comes to you with a new way of thinking, do you instantly go off the deep end? Do you push back with all kinds of knee-jerk reactions? Or can you summon grace and calm that will allow you to pause long enough to get the facts and consider the big picture?

---

33. See Jay Payleitner, *Day-by-Day Devotions for Dads* (Harvest House, 2012), 211–212.

COUNTERING PARENTAL REMARKS

Those who guard their mouths and their tongues keep
themselves from calamity.
—Proverbs 21:23

All parents and grandparents want the children in their family to do great things. Unfortunately, sometimes, things get said that derail their potential excellence before it even has a chance to reveal itself. We go to extremes, either putting on too much pressure or completely minimizing what they're trying to achieve.

Moms and dads may be even guiltier than grandparents. It's not really their fault; it's just that grandparents have a bit more experience as encouragers. It took a while, but we learned when to push and when to ease up. We know what it's like to overwhelm children with our brilliant insight before they even get a chance to test their own approach to a problem. We mistakenly assumed we were supposed to overanalyze every performance, and we end up crushing their teen spirit.

A few examples from past remarks by parents may be instructive. When they ran for class president, we criticized the font on their flyers. When they were already nervous about a clarinet solo, we reminded them of their squeaky performance back in fourth grade. The night before a big cross-country meet, we instructed them to carb up or asked which state-ranked runners they would be competing against. This is all stuff they already knew or didn't help at all.

Parents will probably always be guilty of saying the wrong thing at the wrong time. Their words are reminiscent of the passage in the book of Job in which his three supposed friends, who really didn't understand the situation, arrogantly berated and instructed him instead of offering any kind of empathy. Job replied, *"I have heard many things like these; you are miserable comforters, all of you! Will your long-winded speeches never end? What ails you that you keep on arguing?"* (Job 16:2–3).

When young people are investing themselves in meaningful activities, parents believe they're being helpful when they point out every missed opportunity, imperfection, and potential stumbling block. How might grandparents counterbalance those errant words? First, realize you're all on the same side. Second, in the moment, hold your tongue. If you contradict or reprimand your adult children, they'll be forced to double down on their statements.

Third, take time to process what's going on and formulate words of encouragement that actually encourage. Without contradicting their parents' instruction, you can inject a note of positivity directly to your grandchild. It may be several days later when you say, "Taylor, I can't stop thinking about your concert/play/game/performance the other day. I was so blessed by it. Make sure I get the next one on my calendar. I'm so proud of you."

If you can give specific examples of what you appreciated, even better.

WHAT ABOUT YOU?

Thoughtful grandparents, like you, have all kinds of good advice swirling around in their brain. If you must offer unsolicited advice to your children's parents, gently ask permission. At the right time, say something like, "I have a thought on how to come alongside Jeremy on his big semester project. Can I tell you what I'm thinking?" Then, of course, express positive steps to take, rather than chastising them for things they've said or done. But you knew that, right?

CROSS-GENERATIONAL COMMUNICATION

Ask the former generation and find out what their ancestors learned, for we were born only yesterday and know nothing, and our days on earth are but a shadow.
—Job 8:8–9

While I was working on this devotional, Rita and I were blessed to attend a spiritual retreat for grandparent couples at Glen Eyrie Conference Center in Colorado Springs. Sponsored by Legacy of Faith, the three-day event spent more time than we anticipated—not with strategies on how to connect with grandchildren—but on supporting, encouraging, and communicating with our own adult children in their parenting journey.

Coming alongside and engaging with that next generation might be one of the great unspoken challenges and keys to leaving that legacy we all long for. After all, our adult children are—and should be—the gatekeepers to how much time and interaction we have with their kids. Let's face it: we're not the parents; they are.

Of course, the weekend retreat included valuable spiritual content, but one session focused on how different generations have preferred methods of communication. Not that any generation should be "put in a box." But it's wise to have a general awareness that parents, children, and grandchildren all have different strategies for getting a point across.

For example, the Silent Generation, who came of age and fought World War II, communicated most effectively face-to-face, with handwritten letters, and talking on rotary phones. Famously, veterans who served on the front lines often kept their experiences to themselves, choosing not to communicate much at all.

Baby Boomers engage face-to-face, grew up with extended phone calls, and have taken to both email and Facebook enthusiastically. Just about everyone reading this devotional already gets way too many emails, but we seem to be stuck with it.

Gen X (born 1965–1980) was the first to master technology. As early adapters to email, they still use it in business, but as their parents embraced email and Facebook, they abandoned those platforms as personal options. They prefer text, but you can call in an emergency.

Millennials (born 1981–1996) grew up with video games and live by the code TL;DR. (Too long; didn't read.) More than 92 percent own a smartphone but rarely answer calls! Claiming efficiency, they text. Maybe because their nose is in their phone, they also avoid face-to-face interaction.

All of that leaves our Gen Z and Gen Alpha grandchildren at the mercy of cyberbullying and social media overload. While they may be tech-savvy, their verbal skills are sometimes lacking. Emojis and abbreviations have stifled any writing skills. They also can't write or read cursive. Striving to present a perfect online image, their anxiety is off the charts. Clickbait algorithms have left them opting for speed over substance.

Videochatting is an option, but it requires intentionality and scheduling. Maybe ask your kids to set up a weekly Sunday afternoon group Zoom.

Mostly, grandparents need to be reminded that our goal is not to change the next generation's communication methods but to realize we're living in their world. You may think they're being rude, but they really aren't. Young people are still hungry for connection, so we need to figure out how to enter their lives.

WHAT ABOUT YOU?

In the end, our best communication method might be modeling. Without an avalanche of words, we can still display and teach common courtesy, including how to shake hands, introduce ourselves formally, put down our phones, write thank-you notes, actively listen, make eye contact, and so on. At the Legacy of Faith retreat I mentioned earlier, we were reminded that much of our legacy is caught, not taught. And while your modeling may not translate to immediate behavior modification, the kids are taking it all in.

HOLIDAY RESTORATION
STRATEGIES

The turkey. The sweet potatoes. The stuffing. The pumpkin pie.
Is there anything else we all can agree so vehemently about? I
don't think so.
—Nora Ephron[34]

Lead with love. As a grandparent, that's the best advice you will ever get when approaching a holiday gathering and anticipating tensions, squabbles, sibling rivalry, and hurt feelings among your children, grandchildren, or extended family.

Strategies for applying love are numerous and multifaceted. Patience. Celebrate small victories, such as just getting everyone in the same room. Model humility. Extend grace. Don't add fuel to the fire. Avoid triggers that might lead to giant conflagrations. Reinforce meaningful traditions. Focus on gratitude.

Don't attempt to play referee. You really can't because there are two (or more) sides to each story, and you can't play favorites. If you find yourself in a calm conversation with one of the warring factions, then mostly listen. The most you can probably do is request a favor: "Dear one, this weekend, when we're all together, can you dial down the tension and maybe sprinkle in a little grace?" If that request receives a hint of acceptance, you might even seek out a similar conversation with other relatives who are carrying a grudge.

One hope-filled strategy is to celebrate the youngest members of the family. Even if adult siblings aren't speaking, they can still appreciate the innocent antics of nieces, nephews, younger cousins,

---

34. Nora Ephron, *I Feel Bad About My Neck: And Other Thoughts on Being a Woman* (Alfred A. Knopf, 2006), 6.

and grandkids. Babes in arms, toddlers, and kindergartners can be a distraction and even have a soothing effect on adult tensions.

As the patriarch or matriarch of the family, you are in a unique position to focus on gratitude and God's faithfulness. Even though some members of the next generation may be putting walls up against religion, you can still find winsome ways to bring God into the equation. Although Christian holidays have been largely secularized, the history and meaning of Easter, Thanksgiving, and Christmas remain valid. Don't apologize for giving thanks to the Creator for the turkey and stuffing. Let it be known well ahead of time that you're hoping to fill a pew on Easter morning (and that you're buying brunch afterward). Do all the popular Christmas traditions, making sure to include a group reading from Luke chapter 2.

Again, lead with love.

WHAT ABOUT YOU?

When the kids were growing up, you prayed at meals and as you tucked them in bed. You made church, Sunday school, and youth group a priority. Now, with your empty nest, have you been tempted to de-prioritize church attendance and prayer? You might think that you've put in your time and can go on cruise control with God. One key takeaway from these ninety devotionals could be—on behalf of your children and grandchildren—to double down on your prayer, quiet time, and church involvement.

SEEKING IMMORTALITY

I don't want to achieve immortality through my work. I want to achieve it through not dying.
—Woody Allen[35]

In his classic work *The Brothers Karamazov*, Fyodor Dostoevsky wrote, "If you were to destroy in mankind the belief in immortality, not only love, but every living force maintaining the life of the world would at once be dried up."[36]

Dostoevsky is on to something there. The quest for immortality drives every one of us. There are some who literally attempt to extend their life indefinitely through genetic engineering, cloning, cryogenics, or other questionable scientific methods. Extensive cosmetic surgery is also an ill-advised way to forestall the inevitable.

Creating great art, literature, scientific breakthroughs, or legendary historic achievements can leave a timeless legacy. You might even get a street named after you.

As a grandparent, you've got a third kind of immortality in your sights.

Having kids and watching them have kids—and, if you're so blessed—to watch your kids' kids have kids gives you a unique vision into the future. That idea is reflected in Psalm 103:17: *"But from everlasting to everlasting the LORD's love is with those who fear him, and his righteousness with their children's children."*

35. Mel Gussow, "Everything You Wanted to Know About Woody Allen at 40," *The New York Times*, December 1, 1975, 33.
36. Fyodor Dostoevsky, *The Brothers Karamazov*, trans. Constance Garnett (W. W. Norton & Company, 1976), 70.

In just these few words, the psalmist reminds us that there is an eternity, God's love empowers those who trust in Him, and our grandchildren are also under God's loving care.

That journey of authentic immortality actually begins when each of us—as individuals—understands our own brokenness and need for a Savior, acknowledges that Jesus sacrificed Himself on the cross to pay the penalty for our sins, and accepts that free gift of grace.

Jesus makes this promise in John 5:24: *"Very truly I tell you, whoever hears my word and believes him who sent me has eternal life and will not be judged but has crossed over from death to life."*

I cannot recommend cloning or freezing yourself in that universal quest for eternal life. On the other hand, if you're a scientist or an artist, I do hope your work makes an impact for generations to come. As a sidenote, there's a better chance of that kind of lasting notoriety if your work somehow glorifies God.

When it comes to that third kind of immortality, I join you in prayer that each member of your entire family for generations to come knows and serves the Lord. That would be amazing.

In the end, I hope you've taken care of job one—that is, securing your own place in eternity.

WHAT ABOUT YOU?

Too many people get confused when talking about immortality. They think it's all about making an impact here on earth. But in the last days, *"the earth and everything done in it will be laid bare"* (2 Peter 3:10). On a regular basis, we need to remind ourselves and those we love, "We're not home yet."

A SEASON OF REAPING

*Let us not become weary in doing good, for at the proper time
we will reap a harvest if we do not give up.*
—Galatians 6:9

One of the profound blessings of being a grandparent is witnessing the harvest of seeds sown over many seasons. After years of faithfully pouring love, time, and effort into our families, we are privileged to experience the fruits of our labor in the lives of our grandchildren.

Reaping a harvest doesn't happen by accident.

Throughout our own years of parenting, we faced challenges and moments of uncertainty, wondering if the values, lessons, and faith we instilled in our children would take root. We did our fair share of cultivating, sowing, fertilizing, weeding, praying for rain, pest management, and harvesting. Our own grown children are in the midst of those challenges right now. Perhaps they're stuck in one of those seasons—chasing away locusts or praying for heavenly intervention.

Grandparenting, however, offers a new vantage point. Certainly, on request, you'll want to roll up your sleeves and be the farmhand that works alongside your son or daughter on behalf of your grandchildren. At the same time, your years of gathering wisdom enable you to see signs of growth that active parents often overlook.

Moms and dads have expectations for what kind of fruit will come to harvest. But grandparents might be the first to notice unexpected sprouts, berries, bulbs, and vines in the lives of those young people. What's more, Galatians 6:9 encourages us not to grow weary in doing this work, which gives us permission to continue encouraging, asking the right questions, listening, celebrating, and praising.

Those activities increase the chance that the harvest will be plentiful and rewarding.

A real-life example might be parents steering a child toward one career path when God is calling them to something completely different. There's a good chance that an observant grandparent will notice that seed of potential before anyone else in the family. Including the young upstart themselves!

That kind of healthy harvest comes not from perfection but from perseverance. From not growing weary. All of which makes the reminder to *"not give up"* even more relevant. Call it patience. Call it long-term vision. Call it holding on to hope.

You can and should be an observant, optimistic, and encouraging force on behalf of God's call in the lives of each of your grandchildren.

WHAT ABOUT YOU?

Maybe you didn't realize that the time you spend providing visible expressions of faith and values in your grandchildren helps to cultivate God's call in their lives. Be assured, sharing stories, teaching life lessons, and offering a listening ear are part of the cultivating, sowing, fertilizing, and watering process. But also never forget that Galatians 6:9 reminds us that the harvest comes at *"the proper time,"* in God's time.

DAY 90
THAT DESPERATE HEARTACHE

For I am not ashamed of the gospel of Christ: for it is the power
of God unto salvation to every one that believeth.
—Romans 1:16 (KJV)

We covered this topic earlier, in the devotions for days 24, 25, and 26, but there's so much heartache out there among Christian grandparents that it seems like a fitting—and hopeful—message on which to end our time together.

The number one concern I hear from my audiences is that their grandchildren will not be joining them in heaven.

The desperation is evident. In recent years, too many grandparents have seen their own sons and daughters fade from the church. Growing up, those kids were active in Sunday school and youth group. At home, there were prayers at dinner and bedtime, and engaging spiritual conversations around the kitchen table. Many of those boys and girls—as teenagers or younger—publicly professed their faith and chose baptism.

After they graduated from high school, you saw doubts and worldly cynicism creep in. Choices were made. Words were said. You may have even been told you were old-fashioned, out of touch, or "you just don't get it." It's also possible that many of today's grandparents never witnessed a specific moment when their children turned away from Christ and His church. It just happened.

While this entire ninety-day devotional has been dedicated to nurturing your faith and passing it on, let's confirm three steps you must not miss.

First, be winsome. Commit to living in the light of the fruit of the Spirit. Not just to your grandkids, but to their mom and dad, as well. You may have read, *"Even if some refuse to obey the Good News, your godly lives will speak to them without any words. They will be won over by observing your pure and reverent lives"* (1 Peter 3:1–2 NLT). In this passage, Peter is speaking to wives about living with nonbelieving husbands, but I believe the principle applies to grandparents.

Second, pray. Pray for your grandkids by name. For hearts open to the gospel. For Christian friends to come into their lives. For clear moments when you yourself can love on them and find an opening to share the most important news ever.

Third, which brings us to the most difficult challenge you have: actually delivering the gospel. Your son or daughter and their spouse may have told you in no uncertain terms that they don't want you preaching to their children. For now, those wishes must be honored. But seeds can be planted. You can bear fruit in your own life. You can love on your grandchildren in ways that make them ask, "Papa, how come you're so cool?" Or "Grammy, thanks for all you do."

That's when you can simply respond to those curious and eager minds with your own non-preachy answer: "That's because I have Jesus in my life. Someday, I'll tell you all about Him." Then let the conversation flow naturally.

WHAT ABOUT YOU?

If your adult children don't get up every Sunday to go to church, please don't punish yourself with guilt. If they made a sincere profession of faith in their youth, God can use that to draw them back to Him. If they fell in love with a nonbeliever and are unequally yoked, God can use that, too! As with your grandkids, commit to loving them first and foremost. There's gospel power in your love and prayers.

AFTERWORD

Dear grandparenting friend,

I'm not exactly sure why, but, as I composed these devotions, many times, I found myself in tears. More than I imagined, I came to realize that you and I are on a tremendous journey that has far-reaching implications. In this season of life, being an awesome grandparent is quite likely the very reason God has kept us around.

I can also confirm that God has equipped us with every resource we need to reach our ultimate destination, having completed our mission.

Of course, my heart overflows with love for my children, daughters-in-law, and grandchildren. But—even if we never meet—somehow I have a love in my heart for you and your entire family.

I'm glad we're in this together. Let me know if I can ever serve you in any way, from one caring and hopeful grandparent to another. I'm praying for you. Will you do the same for me?

—Jay (aka Chief)

ABOUT THE AUTHOR

After a decade of penning advertising campaigns for airlines and beer, Jay Payleitner became a freelance radio producer working for Josh McDowell, Chuck Colson, Voice of the Martyrs, Bible League International, and others. He is a popular speaker on grandparenting, parenting, marriage, creativity, and getting life right. Jay has authored more than thirty books, including *The Next Verse, 52 Things Kids Need from a Dad, Checking the Boxes Only You Can Check, Hooray for Grandparents!* and *What If God Wrote Your Bucket List?* Jay is a speaker and creative strategist for Christian Grandparenting Network and partner with Grandkids Matter, Legacy of Faith, Iron Sharpens Iron, and the National Center for Fathering. Jay and his wife, Rita, live near Chicago, where they raised five kids, loved on ten foster babies, and are cherishing grandparenthood. There's more at jaypayleitner.com.

.